TRANSFORMING
PROVIDENCE

TRANSFORMING
PROVIDENCE

Rebirth of a Post-Industrial City

Gene Bunnell

Book cover design by Tracy Fox
Book cover photograph by Richard Benjamin
Copyediting by Rhonda Rosenheck of RE: WORK Editing (reworkediting.com)
Production and printing by Troy Bookmakers (troybookmakers.com)

Planning is a practical activity that is done in places to solve particular problems.... Local allegiances and local perspectives are essential to solving environmental and social problems.

Greg Lindsey

About the Author

Gene Bunnell holds a Master of City Planning degree from the Harvard Graduate School of Design and a Ph.D. in Planning Studies from the London School of Economics and Political Science. He has held faculty appointments at the University of Wisconsin-Madison, and the University at Albany, State University at New York. He has also been a visiting professor at the University of Massachusetts-Amherst, Smith College, Hampshire College and Vassar College. He is the author of *Making Places Special: Stories of Real Places Made Better by Planning* (APA Planners Press 2002) and *Built to Last: A Handbook on Recycling Old Buildings* (Preservation Press 1977). Gene was born and raised in Buffalo, New York.

Contents

List of Abbreviations

APA—American Planning Association
CCC—Capital Center Commission
CDBG—Community Development Block Grant
CETA—Comprehensive Employment and Training Act (Federal)
CNU—Congress for the New Urbanism
CRMC—Coastal Resources Management Council
DPPC—Downtown Providence Parks Conservancy
DPD—Department of Planning and Urban Development, City of Providence
EIS—Environmental Impact Study
FHWA—Federal Highway Administration
FRA—Federal Railroad Administration
GKP—Greater Kennedy Plaza
JDA—Jewelry District Association
JWU—Johnson & Wales University
LISC—Local Initiatives Support Corporation
LEED—Leadership in Energy and Environmental Design
MBTA—Massachusetts Bay Transportation Authority
MOA—Memorandum of Agreement
MOCD—Mayor's Office of Community Development, City of Providence
NEA—National Endowment for the Arts
OPD—Office of Planning and Development, City of Provdence
PawSox—Pawtucket Red Sox
PILOT—Payment in Lieu of Taxes
PRA—Providence Redevelopment Authority
PRF—Providence Revolving Fund
PPS—Providence Preservation Society
RICCA—Rhode Island Convention Center Authority
RIDEM—Rhode Island Department of Environmental Managment
RIEDC—Rhode Island Economic Development Corporation
RIDOT—Rhode Island Department of Transportation
RIPTA—Rhode Island Public Transit Agency
RISD—Rhode Island School of Design
SOM—Skidmore, Owings and Merrill
WBNA—West Broadway Neighborhood Association
URI-CCE—University of Rhode Island, College of Continuing Education

List of Interviews

1998, Ken Orenstein, Executive Director, The Providence Foundation
2015   (1980-1987)

1998   Pete Pointner, Executive Officer, Planning Resources, Inc., Wheaton, IL

1998   Tina Regan, Providence Preservation Society; former chairperson of College Hill Historic District Commission and member of Downcity Design Review Committee

2015   Brent Runyon, Executive Director, Providence Preservation Society

2015   Edward F. Sanderson, Executive Director, State Historic Preservation Officer, Rhode Island Historical Preservation and Heritage Commission

2015   Clark Schoettle, Executive Director, Providence Revolving Fund

1998   Samuel J. Shamoon, Associate Director of Planning, City of Providence

2015   Deming Sherman, Chairman, Capital Center Commission, and former member of Capital Center Design Review Committee

1998   William D. Warner, William D. Warner, Architects and Planners, Exeter, RI

2016   Chrissy Wolpert, Aurora Manager and Director of Programming

2015   Cliff Wood, Executive Director, Downtown Providence Parks Conservancy

2016   Jack Yena, President, Johnson & Wales University (1989-2004)

Preface

During the second half of the 20th century, countless numbers of cities that had prospered as centers of American manufacturing saw their economies progressively undermined and hollowed out by ever-increasing losses in manufacturing employment. Technological changes that rendered previous methods of manufacturing obsolete were responsible for some of the job losses. Cities also lost manufacturing jobs when long-established companies that had been pillars of the local economy decided to relocate to places with lower costs of production. In a broader sense, however, the loss of manufacturing jobs experienced by long-time urban industrial centers was brought about by a fundamental shift of the U.S. economy away from manufacturing and toward being more of a service economy. Bluestone and Harrison (1982) aptly described the disruptive economic restructuring that was taking place in America cities as "the deindustrialization of America."[1]

Cities that suffered the most from deindustrialization were largely concentrated in the Northeast and Midwest. The list of such "rustbelt cities" is a long one, and includes big cities such as Buffalo, Cleveland, Pittsburgh and Detroit, as well as others such as Trenton, New Jersey ("Trenton Makes, the World Takes"); Erie, Reading, Scranton, Allentown and Bethlehem in Pennsylvania; Syracuse and Binghamton in New York; Waterbury and Bridgeport in Connecticut; and Lowell, Lawrence, Haverhill and Worcester in Massachusetts. Providence, Rhode Island, is also on that list.

The economic and psychological dislocation suffered by rustbelt cities due to cascading job losses was, all too often, followed by ill-considered urban renewal clearance projects, undertaken in the vain hope of wiping away reminders of the past, and starting out anew: as if the past were something best forgotten, rather than better used as the foundation for the future. Entire districts and neighborhoods were cleared away, uprooting and displacing long-established businesses and residents—further fracturing the social and economic fabric of communities. The vast tracts of cleared land created in the process often lay vacant for years. When the land was ultimately developed—typically many years later—the development was often mediocre and generic, and did little to enhance the character and vitality of the community. More often than not, the developments that came about were starkly at odds with the historic character that had once provided the basis for local identity and a sense of place.

Unfortunately, most rustbelt cities have continued to languish. A handful, however, have made considerable progress in stabilizing their economies, improving local environmental quality and quality of life, and making themselves more desirable as places to live, work and visit. The rustbelt city that has made by far the most progress in that regard is Providence.

Back in 1998, Providence was being acclaimed as having experienced a renaissance.[2] In April of that year, the American Planning Association held its annual national conference in Boston, and, after attending the conference, I took advantage of Boston's close proximity to Providence, and traveled to Providence to see for myself what had been accomplished, and to interview people who had played key roles in helping bring about the city's transformation. In the succeeding months, I conducted telephone interviews with additional informants, such as with Lachlan Blair and Peter Pointner, who were in Illinois. The findings of this initial research were published as a chapter in *Making Places Special: Stories of Real Places Made Better by Planning* (Bunnell 2002). The chapter on Providence was titled "An Old City Reconnects with Its Past and Finds Its Future."[3]

Upon my joining the faculty of the Department of Geography and Planning at the University at Albany in 2003, I found that the Providence case study in *Making Places Special* provided an excellent way to teach students about effective planning processes and techniques, and community development strategies that can help turn a city around. In 2006, a group of University at Albany graduate urban planning students asked me to lead a study tour of downtown Providence, and the College Hill and Federal Hill neighborhoods. In 2009, I returned to Providence to be the keynote speaker at the West Broadway Neighborhood Association's Annual Meeting. Throughout these years I continued to follow ongoing land use and development issues and initiatives in the city.

Seventeen years after beginning to study Providence, I returned to the city in March 2015 to conduct another round of in-person interviews, and observe how the city had changed in the intervening years. In April 2016, an "Urbanism Summit", organized by the New England chapter of the Congress for the New Urbanism, prompted another return to Providence. Two walking tours offered as part of the conference, one led by Robert Azar, Deputy Director of Planning and Development, and the other by Steve Durkee of Cornish Associates, proved to be especially informative. Between 2015 and 2016, I conducted telephone interviews with additional informants. Plans, planning studies and reports relevant to the changes that had taken place between 1998 and 2016 were obtained and examined, and extensive internet research was conducted.

A total of 30 interviews were conducted. (See the List of Interviews, p. xv for the names and titles of persons interviewed and the years in which they were interviewed.) The personal accounts and perspectives volunteered during these interviews shape the underlying storyline of this book. Frequent quotes drawn from interviews convey a sense of the real-life drama and uncertainty that surrounded many of the local efforts that eventually produced such positive results.

Citizens and elected officials in rustbelt cities elsewhere in the country ought to be especially interested in Providence's experience, and would do well to replicate some of the methods and approaches Providence devised and applied. Finally, and significantly, this book ought to be of interest to people who live and work in and around Providence. My hope is that a shared understanding of how much effort, creativity, and commitment went into in achieving the current gains will inspire citizens to continue to support and participate in local planning processes and initiatives aimed at achieving even more positive outcomes in the future.

Introduction:

Attributes of a Good Place to Live

What are the attributes that make a city a good place to live? I think it makes sense to address that important question before proceeding any further.

Around the time I began the research for *Making Places Special: Stories of Real Places Made Better by Planning* (Bunnell 2002), I came across a book titled *A Good Place to Live—America's Last Migration* by Terry Pindell (1995), in which the author described his personal quest to find a good place to live for himself and his family. The qualities Pindell was seeking turned out to be the same ones I have long valued as an urban planner. This book tells how a number of these same qualities have been strengthened and enhanced in Providence, making Pindell's list of preferred place qualities particularly relevant:

- Local identity and sense of place;

- Strong, vital, densely developed, pedestrian-oriented downtown with a mixture of uses and activities that makes it the focal point of the community;

- Good neighborhoods with well-kept, older housing, adjacent to and surrounding the downtown;

- Gathering places—so-called "third places" that are neither home nor work—where people can interact with one another and have the sense of being part of a larger community;

- Environmental, scenic and open-space resources integrated within the city and/or close at hand.

Chapter One:

History and Background

Providence is one of the oldest cities in the United States. It was first settled in 1636 by a group of people led by Roger Williams, who came to Rhode Island to escape the theologically rigid and repressive Puritan society of the Massachusetts Bay Colony in Salem. They came to Providence in search of change, and established a community based on the principles of religious freedom and the separation of church and state. For that reason, Providence was laid out very differently than were traditional Massachusetts Bay communities. The typical settlement in the Massachusetts Bay Colony was built around a town common, with the established church and meeting house assuming positions of authority overlooking the common. In Providence, there was no established church or town common. Rather, the earliest settlement in Providence involved the laying out of 50 long, narrow lots extending from Town Street (the first public way along Providence River) up what later became known as "College Hill," thereby providing each lot with access to the waterfront (See Figure 1.1). After every fourth lot there was a lane. As the community grew, it became clear that a second public way was needed to supplement Town Street. To meet this need, the proprietors agreed to cut their lots in half, and to establish a new public way about a quarter mile up the hill (parallel to the river and Town Street) that would connect all the lots to one another and enable people and goods to move freely throughout the community. This second public way was given the name "Benefit Street," because it was laid out for the benefit of all the residents of the community.

For roughly 100 years, the settlement remained largely confined to the east side of the Providence River. The area west of the river, where the city's central business and financial districts were eventually built (which Providence residents call "Downcity"), remained undeveloped because the area was surrounded by marshy lowlands and traversed by Muddy Dock Creek, and also hemmed in by the steep Weybosset Hill. Once a bridge was built over the Providence River, however, the area west of the river began to be parceled out and developed. Around 1724, work began on leveling Weybosset Hill, which provided soil to fill in low-lying areas, and clay for brick-making.

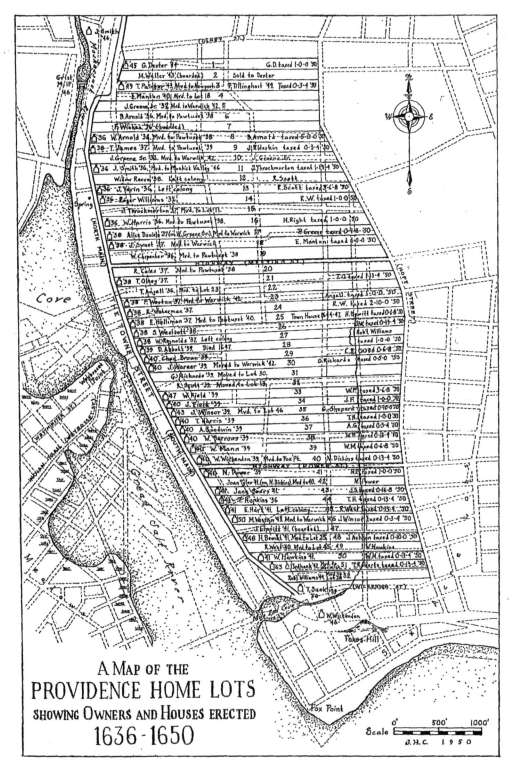

Figure 1.1: Home Lots, College Hill, Providence 1659.
(Source: John Hutchins Cady, *The Civic and Architectural Heritage of Providence*, 1636-1950)

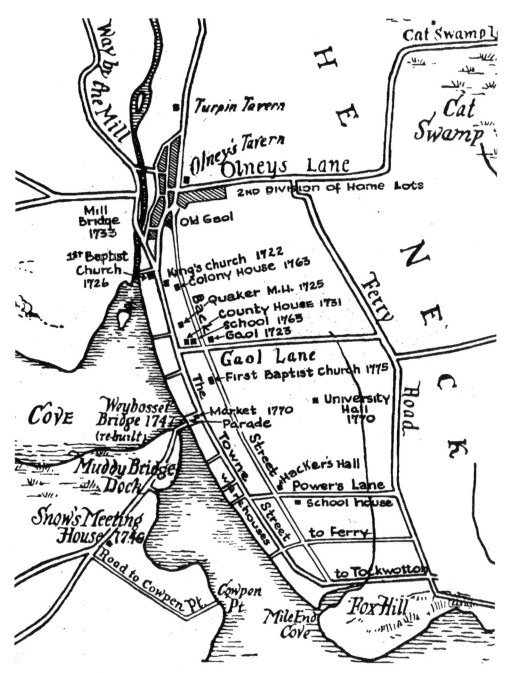

Figure 1.2: Map of Providence *circa* 1775 showing Weybosset Bridge and settlement spreading west across the cove. (Source, John Hutchins Cady, *The Civic Architectural Heritage of Providence*, 1636-1950)

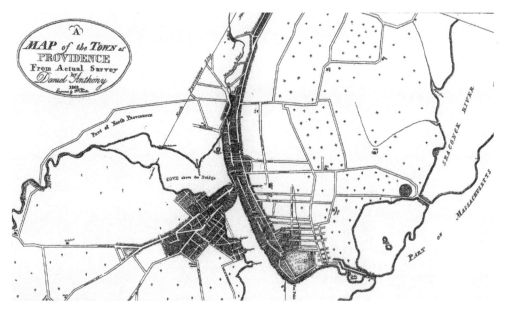

Figure 1.3: Map of Providence in 1803 showing expansion of development on west side of cove. (Source: John Hutchins Cady, *The Civic Architectural Heritage of Providence, 1636-1950*)

Providence remained relatively small and unimportant throughout the 18th century and the first quarter of the 19th century. By 1824, the population of the city was still only about 15,000. Until then, Providence's main claim to fame was that it was a shipping port. However, its harbor was fairly narrow and shallow. As ships grew in size, the city's harbor proved increasingly inadequate, and the bulk of shipping activity gradually shifted to the ports of Boston and New York.

Fortunately for the city, advances in other forms of transportation associated with the Industrial Revolution reinforced its strategic geographic importance. The Boston-to-Providence rail line opened in 1835. A second railroad, running from Providence to Stonington, Connecticut, opened two years later. In 1844, the Providence and Worcester ("P & W") Railroad was established, and an additional rail line was built connecting those two cities. Over time, the center of the city was increasingly claimed for railroad use. A freight yard was developed at the southern terminus of the P & W rail line and a passenger depot was built at Exchange Place in 1848.[4] When the present-day Rhode Island State House was built between 1895 and 1900, it looked out onto railroad tracks and freight yards.

No part of this country was more greatly influenced by the Industrial Revolution than Rhode Island. Major areas of manufacturing that became established in Providence included: cotton textiles; woolen textiles; base metals; the manufacture of machinery and machine tools; and jewelry and silverware. Waves of European immigrants came to Providence and surrounding Rhode Island communities to work in newly built factories.

In 1830 there were 27 jewelry firms employing 280 workers in Providence. By 1850, there were 57 firms with 590 workers. Employment in a number of Providence's industries (other than jewelry) increased significantly during the Civil War. Woolen Mills in Providence supplied tens of thousands of uniforms, overcoats and blankets for federal troops. Metals factories such as Providence Tool, Nicholson and Brownell, and the Burnside Rifle Company provided guns, sabers, and musket parts. Builders Iron Foundry manufactured large numbers of cannons. The Providence Steam Engine Co. built the engines for two Union sloops of war. Congdon and Carpenter supplied the military with hardware such as iron bars, bands, hoops, and horseshoes from its factory at 3 Steeple Street (the city's oldest surviving industrial building).

The postwar economic boom that followed the end of the Civil War brought about unprecedented growth in Providence's jewelry industry. From 45 shops employing over 700 workers in 1865, the industry expanded

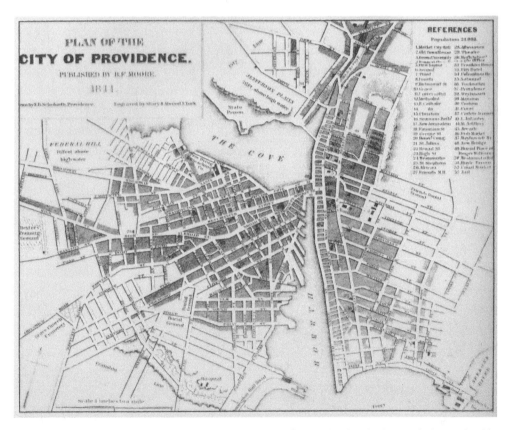

Figure 1.4: As shown in this map of Providence in 1823, settlement by then had expanded considerably west of the Providence River, as well as eastward up College Hill. (Source John Hutchins Cady, *The Civic Architectural Heritage of Providence, 1636-1950*)

to 150 companies with almost 2,700 workers by 1875. By 1880, Rhode Island was the leading state in the manufacture of jewelry, accounting for more than one quarter of the entire national jewelry production. Of the state's 148 firms, 142 of them were in Providence. By 1890, more than 200 Providence firms, employing almost 7,000 workers, were engaged in jewelry manufacture.[5] A large proportion of these firms were located in an area immediately south of the downtown core, which became known as "the Jewelry District."

By 1900, Providence had one of the most powerful and diverse industrial economies of any city in the country. The city contained the world's largest tool factory (Brown and Sharpe), file factory (Nicholson File), engine factory (Corliss Steam Engine Company), screw factory (American Screw), and silverware factory (Gorham), which were proclaimed as Providence's "Five Industrial Wonders" (Conley and Campbell, City Archives).

During the 1920s, employment in Rhode Island's textile industry declined precipitously, as textile manufacturers, especially of cotton goods, left the area in droves and relocated in the South, lured by non-union labor, lower energy costs, lower transportation costs owing to greater proximity to raw materials, and more modern facilities. The city's lone manufacturing bright spot was jewelry manufacturing, where continued growth took up some of the slack created by the decline of the textile industry. The Depression of the 1930s actually stimulated further growth of Providence's jewelry industry, as craftsmen trained in the production of precious jewelry applied their skills to the design of cheaper, mass-produced jewelry.[6]

Downtown Providence traditionally functioned as the center for retail shopping for the region. By 1900, there were three major downtown department stores on or near Westminster Street. The first (the "Boston Store") opened in the early 1870s at the corner of Westminster and Union Streets. The Shepard Co. department store was founded in 1880 and proved so popular that it expanded to occupy an entire city block. The third downtown department store was the Outlet Company, Outlet Company on Weybosset Street, which opened in 1891. Like the Boston Store and Shepard's, the Outlet Company rapidly expanded and, before long, had built a building (168-176 Weybosset Street) that occupied an entire city block. Albert, Peerless, and other department stores did similarly brisk business.

As the 20th century dawned, the future of Providence appeared bright. Not only did it have a vibrant industrial and manufacturing economy; Providence was also the capital of Rhode Island, which provided a solid and reliable core of state government jobs.

Providence moved into the twentieth century with a full head of steam. First in woolen production, third in the manufacture of machinery and machine tools (behind Philadelphia and Cincinnati), and the jewelry capital of the nation... (Conley and Campbell, City Archives).

By 1930, the population of Providence had grown to 253,000. In September 1938, the Great New England Hurricane slammed into southern New England, killing 250 people. Downtown Providence was inundated, submerged under ten feet of water that caused about $120 million in property damage. In 1954, Providence was hit by Hurricane Carol, which brought about a storm surge of eight feet, and caused over $41 million in damage. Insurance companies became understandably hesitant to insure downtown properties, so the cost of insuring them rose significantly. Likewise, banks became loath to write mortgages supporting new investment in downtown. After the 1938 hurricane, no new buildings went up in downtown Providence until construction of the Fox Point Hurricane Barrier was completed in 1966.

By the 1960s, Providence was beginning to suffer from the same negative economic trends that were plaguing other rustbelt cities in the northeast: loss of jobs and population, and consequent disinvestment in inner-city housing stock. The high point in the city's population was attained in 1950, when the population of Providence reached 257,000.

In 1968, the first large suburban shopping mall in Rhode Island opened, in Warwick, only 20 minutes from downtown Providence. It was not long before Downcity retail establishments and department stores began to suffer. The fact that a considerable amount of downtown commercial property was absentee-owned further complicated the situation, and hindered a constructive local response. "A large proportion of downtown properties were held in trust for absentee owners who simply collected their monthly checks and did little else," stated Ken Orenstein (1998 int.).

A City Severed by Rail Lines and Interstate Highways

When railroads were first built through Providence, little thought was given to the effects their rights-of-way might have on the livability and efficient functioning of the city. Civic and business leaders in Providence were all too happy to approve whatever alignment the railroad companies considered most cost-effective and advantageous. As a result, an elevated railroad corridor twelve tracks wide was built through the city's downtown, separating Downcity from the State House and surrounding areas.

Likewise, when highway engineers began laying out interstate highways through Providence, they did so with a single purpose in mind, with little consideration of the negative impacts the chosen alignment could have downtown and in adjoining neighborhoods. Interstate highways built through Providence in the 1960s cut wide swaths through the city. Construction of Interstate 195, completed in 1968, effectively eviscerated the Jewelry District, and Interstate 95 was placed in a trench that cut off the city's West Side from its downtown.

Figure 1.5: Downtown Providence in October 1949, with the Rhode Island State House overlooking railroad tracks and freight yards. (Source: The Providence Journal)

NORTH-SOUTH FREEWAY, DECEMBER 1960

Figure 1.6: Interstate highways being constructed through Providence, 1960. (Source: Providence Department of Planning and Development)

Chapter Two:

Saving a Neighborhood— the First Step in Saving the City

It is both wonderful and incredible that it happened the way it did.
—Tina Regan

By the 1950w, the College Hill neighborhood, one of the most historically significant areas in Providence, had become one of the worst slums in the city, an area of badly run-down and overcrowded tenements. Five and six families lived in each tenement. Mostly, heat was delivered by space heaters, and it was common for one basement bathroom to serve an entire building.

Ironically, some of the forces that contributed to the destabilization and decline of College Hill came from the venerable educational institutions located there. It was largely Brown University's heavy-handed institutional expansion that prompted the formation of the Providence Preservation Society (PPS) in 1957. PPS was initially formed for the sole purpose of preserving the College Hill neighborhood. As planner Lachlan F. Blair succinctly put it, "Brown was the devil."

During the 1950s and 1960s, under a new president, Brown University was intent on expanding and began acquiring property on which to build new university buildings and parking lots. One historic building after another on the edge of the campus was demolished, and large-scale buildings, of modern design that clashed with the intimate scale and historic character of the surrounding neighborhood, began to rise on cleared sites.[7] Property acquisitions and demolitions conducted by Rhode Island School of Design (RISD) further destabilized the neighborhood. In the fall of 1959, RISD demolished the historic Pearce House at 225-227 Benefit Street, despite receiving offers from individuals associated with the Providence Preservation Society to purchase and restore it. An article in *The Providence Journal*, published on September 30, 1959, quoted John R. Frazier, president of RISD, as saying that the school could see no alternative to removing the building, and was not interested in selling or leasing the property to outside interests.

The future of the College Hill neighborhood was threatened from yet another direction. In the 1950s and 1960s, many American cities undertook federally funded urban renewal projects that led to the clearance of large portions of their downtowns. Inner-city neighborhoods were designated as "blighted" and cleared away. As Tina Regan put it when I interviewed her in 1998, "Here was this run-down neighborhood that was essentially part of the downtown, and also right next to old industrial buildings and warehouses. Here comes this tool called 'urban renewal,' that could clear away the clutter and all these blighted buildings." Indeed, it seemed altogether likely at the time that the urban renewal land acquisition and clearance activities that had already begun downtown (the Weybosset area had already been bulldozed) would extend into the College Hill neighborhood.

Figure 2.1: Historic home across from a gate to the campus of Brown University being stripped of building materials prior to its demolition. (Source: *The Providence Journal*)

Figure 2.2: Historic residential structure at 225-227 Benefit Street, just before falling to the wreckers' hammers. The structure was demolished by the Rhode Island School of Design despite the Providence Preservation Society's pleas that it be preserved. (Source: *The Providence Journal*)

The Way College Hill Used to Be

When interviewed in 1998, Tina Regan had been a member of the Providence Preservation Society (PPS) for 23 years, had served as chairperson of the College Hill Historic District Commission and as a member of the Downcity Design Review Committee, and had staffed the Preservation Society's office on Meeting Street.

Ms. Regan began by making clear that the College Hill neighborhood of 1998 was a very different place than it was back in the 1950s and 1960s. "When I came from the west side to take art lessons on Saturday mornings at RISD, here on College Hill, my mother made it a point of always saying as I went out the door, 'Don't go down Benefit Street'—which should give you a pretty good idea of what it had become."

Tina recalled going to public meetings at which large-scale clearance schemes were presented; she got the impression that the people in charge of them had no clear vision of the kind of city they wanted to create, once everything was cleared away. "The main impression I got was that the people who were administering urban renewal in Providence back then had no training or background in planning a city, and really didn't know what to do with all the urban renewal money they were getting. They knew there was an opportunity to do something big, but really had no idea what the end-product was going to be or how to bring it about."

During the 1950s and 1960s, Providence had a citizen-member Planning Commission, and a small planning staff headed by Frank Malley, who was an engineer rather than an urban planner. The Planning Commission was ostensibly responsible for the overall planning of the city; however, the real power over land use and development resided in the Providence Redevelopment Agency (PRA), which had a large staff of its own and was focused on carrying out urban-renewal-style clearance projects. It wasn't until the early 1970s that Mayor Joseph Doorley established a Department of Planning and Urban Development (DPUD), and folded the responsibilities of the PRA into that new city department (thereby making the DPUD director also the director of the PRA).

If urban renewal and highway building had not had such a devastating effect on Providence, Tina Regan probably would not have become involved in the fight to save College Hill. But she saw what urban renewal and interstate highway building had done to the West Side, where she lived. She knew there had to be a better way of remaking the city.

Ms. Regan became active in the Providence Preservation Society and joined the College Hill effort in 1975, after the College Hill Plan had been prepared and midway through the process of implementing its recommendations. The people, she says, who deserve the most credit for reviving College Hill were long-time College Hill residents, such as John Nicholas Brown, Beatrice "Happy" Chace, Elizabeth G. Allen, Frances S. Sloan, Mary Elizabeth Sharpe, and others, who, with the help and guidance of architectural historian Antoinette F. Downing, initiated and carried out a remarkably successful planning effort.[8] The goal these people had in mind was not merely to *stop* something from happening, but rather to *bring about positive changes* within the College Hill neighborhood.

From the beginning, organizers and leaders of the community-driven effort emphasized the importance of planning, and of developing a coherent, overall strategy rather than simply pursuing a series of *ad hoc*, crisis-driven actions. They did not simply speak out *against* the plans of Brown and the city; they put forward a positive message of their own. In the words of Tina Regan, "They said, 'We have to slow down. We have to develop a plan and carry that plan through.'" Over time, professional planners and architects became more involved and played increasingly important roles. The first "outside" consultant to be brought in was Lachlan F. Blair, who was hired to help the group write an application for a "demonstration planning grant" from the Housing and Home Finance Agency of the U.S. Urban Renewal Administration. Prior to founding a private consulting firm along with Stewart Stein in 1957, Blair had been state planning chief for the State of Rhode Island, and deputy planning director of the City of Providence. The application was successful, and the demonstration planning grant of $40,000 was matched by an additional $20,000 raised by the Providence Preservation Society. Blair's newly established consulting firm got the job.

Blair and Stein were responsible for directing the overall planning effort, the purpose of which was to document and describe significant historic and architectural resources and to develop a detailed plan and implementation strategy for the area. To accomplish that, they assembled an interdisciplinary team of professionals, including architectural historian Antoinette F. Downing and architect/planner William D. Warner. Another person drawn into the project was Martin Adler, who had just earned a Master's degree in planning and was awarded a student internship from the American Society of Planning Officials to work on the College Hill project.[9]

The next step Blair and Stein took was to study, and learn from, the experience of other cities that had been leaders in preservation planning. This helped the team generate ideas concerning how they would approach their task in Providence. "It also helped us avoid the mistakes that others had made," Blair pointed out. Cities that had conducted surveys of historic buildings, and/or had adopted city ordinances regulating land use and structures in historic areas, were identified and studied. [10]

Antoinette F. Downing, a tenacious advocate of historic preservation and highly respected scholar in the field, also became increasingly involved in a professional-consultant capacity.[11] It was Downing who developed the survey tools and methods that were used in College Hill—including a system of categories to classify and describe properties, and a numerical system to rate properties in terms of their historic significance—as well as the actual survey forms that were used in the field.

After conducting the survey and analyzing the results, and after a thorough study of the neighborhood (including an analysis of traffic, parking, institutional land uses, public schools and open space), a final report was prepared. The writing of the final report, like the conduct of the entire planning process, was a team effort. The report, titled *College Hill: A Demonstration Study and Plan for Historic Area Renewal* ("the 1959 College Hill plan"), was over 200 pages long and contained scores of maps, photographs, and illustrations.

The first section of the 1959 College Hill plan, titled "Preservation Elsewhere," was largely written by Blair and provided a succinct but thorough overview of preservation efforts in other cities throughout the U.S. The second part of the report, written primarily by Downing, described the history of College Hill and the various architectural styles associated with different periods in the area's development. Techniques used in surveying the area's architectural and historic resources, criteria used in judging the historic significance of buildings, and the methodology used for assigning scores to buildings (*i.e.*, taking into account their physical condition and the degree of alteration), were also described.

The third and final part of the report, written by Warner, addressed the question, "What should and can be done?" In this section, detailed proposals for nine different sub-areas within College Hill were presented, and tied together into what was called a "25-Year Plan." The recommended implementation strategy was multifaceted, calling for actions to be taken on a number of different levels:

- Establish a permanent committee or organization to guide and oversee development efforts related to the 1959 College Hill plan;

- Undertake an urban renewal project in the College Hill area including selective clearance, rehabilitation and conservation, as well as public infrastructure improvements;

- Establish an historic trail along Benefit Street;

- Develop a national historic park at the site of the Roger Williams Spring on North Main Street;

- Adopt special zoning regulations for the protection of the historic area of College Hill (the 1959 College Hill plan included proposed state-enabling legislation authorizing the establishment of historic districts and adoption of historic district zoning);

- Stimulate private investment in College Hill by alerting individuals and groups to opportunities for investment in the area;

- Urge institutions of higher education located in the College Hill area to be guided by the recommendations contained in the 1959 College Hill plan, and to cooperate with the city and with each other when planning for the physical development of their campuses;

- Plant street trees in renewal areas designated for rehabilitation, particularly along the "Benefit Street Trail;"

- Adopt and enforce municipal regulations related to zoning and housing codes;

- Undertake carefully planned publicity, education, and information programs to increase public understanding of and support for the aims of the 1959 College Hill plan.

Lachlain Blair said that many people had told him that one of the most important things to come out of the College Hill effort was *a structured methodology for inventorying and evaluating historic properties*. In fact, the building form and methodology used at College Hill were subsequently adopted by the National Trust for Historic Preservation, and have been used across the country as the basis for surveying and inventorying properties for historic district designation. In Blair's opinion, what happened at College Hill provides two other important lessons: "First, it demonstrated the importance of structuring a task. Second, it demonstrated that planning and preservation go hand in glove."

The Impact of the College Hill Plan

One year after the 1959 College Hill plan was completed, the city passed an Historic District zoning ordinance, creating the College Hill Historic District and establishing the College Hill Historic District Commission. Under the ordinance, the commission was given some extremely important powers to safeguard historic buildings in the district. No building in the district could be demolished and no exterior remodeling or alteration of any building in the district could take place without the specific permission of the commission.

It did not take long for the power and resolve of the commission to be tested. RISD came before them seeking permission to tear down the Woods-Gerry mansion at 62 Prospect Street, built in 1860. The college argued that the building was run-down and needed to be demolished to accommodate future college expansion.

In an attempt to find a compromise, the commission found a person willing to repair the house and live in it, if the college would give him a 20-year lease. The college said no and forced the issue to a vote. Antoinette Downing, who chaired the College Hill Historic District Commission, recalled in a 1979 newspaper interview that, when she went to the climactic meeting at which the vote was to be taken, she was so uncertain of the outcome that she had prepared a minority opinion. The vote of the commission turned out to be unanimous and the demolition application was turned down.

Because a revered local college was the applicant, and the case represented the first test of the commission's powers, the commission's decision was controversial. However, public acceptance of the commission's role in regulating actions affecting properties in the historic district has grown considerably over time. For many years, RISD did nothing with the Woods-Gerry Mansion. Eventually, however, the college restored the mansion. Today, it houses RISD's Admissions Office and an art gallery.

Figure 2.3: Woods-Gerry mansion, now serving as the Admissions Office of RISD and an art museum (Source: Gene Bunnell)

Two years after the College Hill plan was completed, a report was prepared and issued documenting the progress that had been made in implementing the plan's various recommendations. The report, titled *College Hill 1961—progress after planning* ("the 1961 College Hill report"), was prepared by Martin Adler. There were two reasons for preparing the report. First, because the 1959 College Hill plan had called for conserving most of the existing fabric of the neighborhood, people might not recognize the subtle and gradual changes that had taken place. Reminding people of what had been accomplished was also seen as a way of building public support for carrying through with the rest of the program.

According to the 1961 College Hill report, the following actions called for in the 1959 College Hill plan had been implemented:

- A 20-member College Hill Coordinating Committee had been organized to oversee the implementation of the plan.

- A federally assisted, preservation-oriented urban renewal program had begun in the College Hill area; those deteriorated properties that did not significantly contribute to the character of the neighborhood had been cleared.

- A state-enabling act for historic area zoning had been enacted in 1959, and an historic district zoning ordinance was adopted for the College Hill area in 1960. A seven-member historic district commission had also been established to administer and enforce the provisions of the historic district zoning ordinance.

- The Providence Preservation Society had developed educational materials and maps related to the Benefit Street Historic Trail (also called the "Historic Mile"), and guided tours of the College Hill area had been organized and conducted to enhance public appreciation of the architectural and historic resources of the area.

- Legislation had been drafted and submitted for congressional approval establishing a national historic park along the western edge of College Hill, at the site of the spring which provided water for Roger Williams and his settlers.

- Private individuals and corporations had bought approximately 30 pre-1840 houses with the intention of restoring them.

- The Episcopal Diocese of Rhode Island had acquired three houses on Benefit Street, and restored and converted them into apartments for the elderly.

A great deal had been accomplished in a relatively short period of time. Nevertheless, the neighborhood still looked generally run- down. In the minds of realtors, developers and bankers, and prospective homebuyers, College Hill remained a risky place in which to invest. Because of these perceived risks (which were made worse by the precariousness of the downtown real estate market, just across the river), few people were prepared to buy run-down College Hill properties, and then spend the considerable sums required to restore them and make them livable.

Beatrice "Happy" Chace refused to sit on the sidelines and allow historic properties to continue to deteriorate. Chace was a long-time resident of Providence, a founding member of the Providence Preservation Society, and a strong supporter of the College Hill planning process. To save many of the oldest homes in the city, Chace formed the Burnside Corporation in the 1960s, purchased several dozen houses (primarily in the block bounded by Benefit, Jenckes, Halsey and Pratt streets), and proceeded to restore their exteriors. She also had new, infill housing built on Pratt Street, on land that had been cleared of severely deteriorated structures.

Figure 2.4: Restored homes on Benefit Street. (Source: Gene Bunnell)

Ms. Chace had hoped that the renovated exteriors of the historic properties she owned, and the dramatically improved appearance of the area, would entice people to want to buy them, renovate their interiors and live in them. Still, few people stepped forward to buy the properties Ms. Chace had rescued. For many years, Ms. Chace continued to own and maintain a large number of properties in the College Hill area, waiting for others to follow.

It is impossible to over-estimate the significance of what "Happy" Chace did and its importance in helping to fulfill the aims of the 1959 College Hill plan. Had she not stepped forward to invest in College Hill when the market for property in the neighborhood was extremely weak, the physical renewal of College Hill would undoubtedly have taken much longer—and might not have happened at all.

In 1967, a second edition of the 1959 College Hill plan was published that included an additional section. Part IV of the second edition, titled "Progress Since 1959," reported on the progress that had been made over an eight-year period in implementing the nine key actions recommended in the 1959 College Hill plan. It reported that an urban renewal program had been formulated for the area by the PRA that was substantially as recommended in the original report. It also reported that progress was being made in creating Roger Williams Spring National Park on a site bounded by Canal Street, Smith Street, Park Row and North Main Street, and that the National Parks Service was conducting a study to estimate the total cost of the project, including the cost of moving the Thomas Clemence House (circa 1680) to the site to serve as the Visitors' Center. The site was placed on the National Register of Historic Places in 1966.

Figure 2.5: Roger Williams Spring National Park (Source: Gene Bunnell)

Figure 2.6: Visitor Center, Roger Williams Spring National Park—a good place for first-time visitors to stop by before setting out to explore the historic College Hill neighborhood. (Source: Gene Bunnell)

Roger Williams Spring National Park has been a marvelous addition to the urban fabric of Providence. The 4.5 acre park overlooking the Moshassuck River buffers the College Hill neighborhood from the Capital Center development area on the other side of the river. The park also provides a visual amenity for people living in the row of Capital Center apartment buildings on the opposite side of the river that look out onto it.

A map was included in the 1967 edition of the College Hill plan that identified 28 properties that had burned or been torn down in the years that followed adoption of the neighborhood's Historic District zoning ordinance in 1956. In an effort aimed at encouraging more people to be willing to purchase and restore historic old homes, the Providence Preservation Society organized a Consultant Bureau composed of professionals who volunteered to supply expert advice and guidance upon request.

Reconciling Neighborhood and Institutional Interests

A regulatory mechanism was eventually established to help avoid the intense conflicts that were sparked when Brown University and RISD acquired and demolished buildings without regard for the effect such actions would have on the surrounding neighborhood. The 1959 College Hill plan had specifically addressed this problem by recommending that "the Rhode Island

School of Design, Brown University and Bryant College work jointly with the Providence City Planning Commission to plan the future growth of the community and the institutions." In an action that met the spirit and intent of that recommendation, the city's planning department drafted and the City Council adopted a special institutional overlay zoning district in 1986, which imposed special requirements and obligations on the city's seven major colleges and seven hospitals, over and above those specified by the underlying, pre-existing zoning.

The boundaries of the new institutional overlay zoning district were drawn to conform exactly to the boundaries of the city's institutions *as they existed in 1986.* In effect, the new zoning ordinance declared that universities or hospitals were allowed in areas where they currently existed, but were prohibited outside those areas. The only way universities or hospitals could expand in the future was to request that adjoining properties be rezoned to be included in the institutional zone: and that meant coming before the City Council and having a public hearing that neighborhood people could attend. At the same time, the city also adopted a "master plan" requirement that called upon colleges and hospitals to prepare and file a master plan as a public document with the city. "It was basically a disclosure statement designed to inform the city of what they intended to do, so that we could plan for it as well" (Shamoon int.).

Simply requiring institutions to "disclose" their plans ultimately proved insufficient to achieve the intent of the ordinance. In 1991, a revised master plan requirement was therefore adopted requiring institutions to prepare a formal, printed master plan document, and submit it to the City Plan Commission for its approval, which could only be given after a formal public hearing on the plan is held. Furthermore, the institutions were required to prepare and file updated master plans every five years, and each time go through the process of holding a public hearing and gaining City Plan Commission approval.

Institutional master plans must contain certain specified elements. For example, each plan must provide a complete inventory (by location) of all properties owned by the institution, with a description of each building and each property's use. It must also describe anticipated facility changes and construction projects, and identify specific areas into which the institution expected to expand in the next five years.

Twenty-five years later, the institutional master plan requirements remain in force, helping to minimize conflicts like those that arose when local colleges and institutions kept their intentions secret, and acted unilaterally without consulting with their neighboring communities.

College Hill Today

Hundreds of historically and architecturally significant structures in the College Hill neighborhood have been restored, and a unique, inner-city neighborhood has been stabilized and revived. As a result, residents of Providence are presented with an opportunity to live in a distinctive urban neighborhood very different from the neighborhoods most Americans typically experience. Over 11,000 people live in the College Hill neighborhood, only "a stone's throw" away from the heart of the city.

Below are three examples of the exquisite, uniquely designed historic structures that can be found in the College Hill neighborhood.

Because most of College Hill's streets were laid out long before the automobile age, they are relatively narrow and parking spaces can be hard to find. People who have grown accustomed to having private driveways, and two- and three-car garages, would probably not want to live there. Also, lots tend to be relatively small with buildings fairly close together, so people who want large private yards and nothing to do with their neighbors probably won't want to live in College Hill. College Hill is a densely developed, congested place. On the other hand, for people who want to live in a unique and stimulating urban environment, who value history and architecture, and like to walk, there could hardly be a better place.

In many American cities, the gentrification of neighborhoods and the

Figure 2.7: This view looking out over roofs of College Hill homes conveys a sense of the close proximity of the College Hill neighborhood to downtown (Source: Gene Bunnell)

Figure 2.8: Joseph Brown House (1774) at 40 South Main Street. (Source: Gene Bunnell)

resulting displacement of low- and moderate-income persons has become a serious concern. Some people might, therefore, criticize what was achieved at College Hill by observing that restoring the neighborhood may very well have displaced low-income people who occupied its badly run-down but cheap tenements. Even more widespread displacement, however, would have occurred if the College Hill preservation plan not been prepared and implemented. The years of disinvestment that would have inevitably resulted from a policy of benign neglect would have resulted in widespread loss of deteriorated structures due to abandonment and fire, and eventually made urban-renewal-driven clearance of the area almost unavoidable. More of College Hill's housing stock has been preserved than just elegant homes for wealthy people. Multi-unit residential structures, with various-sized housing units capable of meeting the needs of different types and sizes of households, have likewise been preserved. Many people who live in College Hill are well-off economically, but the neighborhood population is remarkably varied in terms of income, age, and household characteristics. Indeed, over one-quarter of the people who live in the College Hill neighborhood are students.

Figure 2.9: Providence Institution for Savings, Old Stone Bank (1854, 1898), 86 South Main Street. (Source: Gene Bunnell)

Figure 2.10: From left to right: Fleur-de-lys Studios (1885), 7 Thomas Street; Seril Dodge House I (1786-1906), 10 Thomas Street; and Seril Dodge House II (1791, 1886), 11 Thomas Street (now the Providence Art Club). (Source: Gene Bunnell)

Chapter Three:

Preservation Efforts Expand
to Neighborhoods Beyond College Hill

During its early years as an organization, the Providence Preservation Society focused its attention almost exclusively on College Hill, and expended little if any effort on encouraging the preservation and restoration of structures in neighborhoods and districts outside that somewhat limited area. In 1972, Deborah Dunning was hired as the organization's new Executive Director. Dunning recalls that when she was interviewed for the Executive Director position, she asked: "Do you think the Providence Preservation Society should do more to live up to its name, by extending its preservation efforts throughout the city rather than limiting them to just College Hill?" (Dunning int.).

In the years that followed Dunning's hiring, PPS did indeed begin to devote greater attention to nurturing preservation initiatives in other parts of the city. In 1977, PPS secured a grant from the National Endowment for the Humanities to bring leaders from other parts of the country to Providence, to share how preservation had helped revitalize their cities. Lee Adler told about preservation successes brought about by Savannah's Preservation Revolving Fund. Arthur Skolnick spoke about the revitalization of Seattle's historic Pioneer Square Historic District. Inspired and energized by what they heard from Adler and Skolnick, PPS began to consider the possibility of establishing a Neighborhood Revolving Fund in Providence.

Establishing the Neighborhood Revolving Fund

After researching how to set up the Revolving Fund, PPS decided to establish the entity as a 501(c)(3) corporation, separate from PPS, but with overlapping membership. A 13-member Board of Directors was established for the fund, which included PPS's executive director and board chair. The Revolving Fund secured a challenge grant of $150,000 from the Rhode Island Foundation for initial capitalization, and Mayor Cianci committed $300,000 in Community Development Block Grant Funds over five years to augment the available funding. An additional $750,000 was borrowed from the State-wide Revolving Loan Fund.

In 1981, Wendy Nicholas became Executive Director of PPS. The organization's neighborhood outreach efforts increased considerably with the hiring of Joan Rich as PPS's first neighborhood coordinator (Nicholas int.). An important result was the establishment of the West Broadway Neighborhood Association (WBNA), which had previously operated as the West Broadway Homeowners Association.[12] With funding provided by PRF, a former Texaco gas station on Westminster Street was purchased and renovated for use as WBNA's headquarters.

In 1983, Clark Schoettle became Executive Director of the Providence Revolving Fund. When I interviewed him in 2015, Schoettle was still working in that capacity: a veteran of a 32-year period during which the Revolving Fund had made $9.5 million in loans for 425 projects, saved 15 buildings on PPS's "Most Endangered" list, and leveraged $110 million in private investment. Loan defaults during that period totaled only $155,000.

As of 2015, there was roughly $2.8 million in the Neighborhood Revolving Fund. According to Schoettle, the Fund was able to borrow money from the Rhode Island Foundation at 1% interest, and loaned out the money at 5% interest. "So if all goes well," he explained, "the Fund makes a small profit on each transaction, which adds to the amount of money that can be loaned out later" (Schoettle int.).

Over time, the Revolving Fund's measured and steady approach to rescuing distressed properties has had a considerable impact.

> In any given year we tend to make about 10 loans to help existing homeowners renovate and upgrade their properties. Our approach is incremental, and we engage neighborhood residents in the process of screening projects. By renovating 10 homes per year for more than 30 years we've brought about the renovation of more than 300 homes. We tend to target our activities on particular neighborhoods—such as the Armory District, the Elmwood neighborhood and South Providence (Schoettle int.).

In addition to making loans to homeowners who want to renovate their properties, the Revolving Fund also typically acquires, renovates and eventually resells one building per year. For example, the Revolving Fund has bought run-down, abandoned three-family homes to renovate, converting them into two-family structures, with the homebuyer typically occupying two floors and a rental unit on one.

Figure 3.1: 18-20 Hammond Street, Before. (Source: Providence Revolving Fund)

Figure 3.2: 18-20 Hammond Street, After. (Source: Providence Revolving Fund)

Figure 3.3: 56 Wesleyan Avenue, Before. (Source: Providence Revolving Fund)

Figure 3.4: 56 Wesleyan Avenue, After. (Source: Providence Revolving Fund)

Figure 3.5: 68 Hudson Street, Before. (Source: Providence Revolving Fund)

Figure 3.6: 68 Hudson Street, After. (Source: Providence Revolving Fund)

Figure 3.7: 99 Comstock, Before. (Source: Providence Revolving Fund)

Figure 3.8: 99 Comstock, After. (Source: Providence Revolving Fund)

Figure 3.9: 377-381 Broadway, Before. (Source: Providence Revolving Fund)

Figure 3.10: 377-381 Broadway, After. (Source: Providence Revolving Fund)

Figure 3.11: 576 Broadway, Before. (Source: Providence Revolving Fund)

Figure 3.12: 576 Broadway, After. (Source: Providence Revolving Fund)

The staff of the Revolving Fund includes two contractor/architects, who prepare all the plans and contract documents; thus, it need not hire outside architects. "We also don't use big contractors on our projects," explained Schoettle. "We use neighborhood-based builders, who are scrappier. As a result, we can do projects relatively inexpensively for under $100 per square foot." When the renovation is completed and the Revolving Fund sells the building, it typically places a 30-year deed restriction, limiting the property's resale price in order to assure that the affordability made possible by the fund's subsidy is maintained. It also imposes an easement in perpetuity on the property, which protects the building from demolition or improper alterations.[13] Properties that have been renovated using federal funds for affordable housing are subject to an easement requiring that the units remain affordable to households with 60 - 80% of the area's median income for 15-30 years.[14]

One place where the Revolving Fund has made a markedly positive impact is the Armory District neighborhood. The Revolving Fund partnered with for-profit developers Mark Van Noppen and B.J. Dupre, who were urban pioneers in the 1970s and 1980s. Working in tandem with them in the Armory District over a two-year period, the Revolving Fund acquired and renovated three buildings, and Van Noppen and Dupre renovated another three buildings, which together had a huge impact, jump-starting further, more widespread renovation efforts.

Chapter Four:

Downtown Hits Bottom

The 1961 Downtown Plan

Two years after the 1959 College Hill plan was prepared, as conditions in downtown Providence were becoming increasingly bleak, the PRA prepared a plan called *Downtown Providence 1970—A Master Plan for Downtown Providence* ("the 1961 Downtown plan").[15] The Federal Urban Renewal Administration funded two-thirds of the $165,000 cost of preparing the plan. The plan was fairly typical of the urban renewal plans that were being prepared in other cities during the 1960s, in that it called for widespread clearance within the downtown area and for the construction of major new highways into and through the city. "Bird's-eye" view illustrations in the document showed vast areas of surface parking, new parking garages, and modern, high-rise office buildings. The main purpose of the plan appears to have been to make it easier for people to drive cars into the city, park, and then drive out again. The one exception was the plan's call for closing Westminster Street and converting it to a pedestrian mall: which was actually done in the mid-1980s, with disastrous results.

Other than closing Westminster to traffic, very little of what was called for in that plan was executed. However, there was *one* major planning idea in the 1961 Downtown plan that did exert a powerful influence in reshaping the city in the future: the idea of relocating the mainline railroad tracks and moving them closer to the State House.

The 1974 Interface Providence Plan

Thirteen years after the 1961 Downtown plan was completed, a second downtown plan was independently prepared by a team of faculty members at RISD led by Gerald Howes. A grant from the National Endowment for the Arts provided funding to prepare the plan.[16] The plan, titled *Interface Providence* (the "1974 Interface Providence plan"), was prepared at the height of the "Arab oil embargo" imposed by the Organization of Petroleum Exporting

Countries (OPEC). As the price of gasoline soared, and as motorists found it increasingly difficult to find gas stations where they could fill up their tanks, conserving energy became an increasingly important public concern. One of the main purposes of the 1974 Interface Providence plan, therefore, was to promote energy conservation by encouraging people to make greater use of public transportation.

To achieve that aim, the plan called for an intermodal transportation center to be built next to the Union Railroad Station: which would make it easier to transfer from trains to bus transit, and vice versa, and encourage people to rely less on automobiles. What the 1974 plan did *not* foresee was that a new railroad station would eventually be developed away from the Old Union Station in conjunction with the relocation of the Northeast Rail Corridor.

In retrospect, the most important recommendation in the 1974 Interface Providence plan was that the city should recapture its waterfront by uncovering the rivers that flowed through the downtown. Years later, this key idea resurfaced and became a cardinal element in a visionary plan for transforming downtown Providence.

Vincent A. Cianci, Jr. Enters the Picture

Figure 4.1: Buddy Cianci and the city he loved (Source: AP Images)

Vincent "Buddy" Cianci, Jr., began his first term in office as Mayor of Providence in January 1974, at a truly dark time in the city's economic history. "When he first took office … Providence was in the depths of a seemingly terminal downward slide" (Gourevitch, 2002, 106). That same year, the 18-story Biltmore Hotel, which had served as the city's flagship hotel for over 50 years, closed its doors, dealing a devastating blow to the city's collective psyche.

Cianci was Providence's mayor for a total of twenty-one years—with two noteworthy interruptions. In 1984, he pleaded *nolo contendere* and was forced to resign from office over charges that he had assaulted an acquaintance of his who was having an affair with his wife. In 1991, Cianci was elected mayor a second time. Ten years later, in 2001, he was charged with 37 federal counts that ran ranged from extortion to bribery to racketeering. Convicted on the charge of racketeering, Cianci was forced to resign in 2002. However, he remained characteristically feisty and unrepentant, and continued to insist that he was not a crook. "I was found guilty of being mayor (*ibid.,* 118)."

By all accounts, Cianci was one of the most skilled, charismatic political figures to ever hold public office in Rhode Island; but there were clearly other sides to his character that presented a more complicated and somewhat unsettling picture.

> Short, compact and faintly menacing, Mr. Cianci walked about Providence with the swagger of a man who left his imprint on the skyline and even the pavement of the city. But his strutting could never quite shake the tragic air that enveloped him: a gregarious man who seemed lonely; a supremely gifted politician whose ego and foibles had brought him low, a walking coulda-been (Barry 2016, A22).

Cianci spent four and a half years in federal prison. After his release from prison in 2007, he re-inserted himself into the public life of the city by hosting a radio show and being a frequent guest commentator on television. In 2014, the 73-year-old Cianci announced he wanted his job back as Mayor of Providence, and would campaign as an independent. This time, voters in Providence denied him another chance.

The twenty-eight-year period (1974-2002) spanned by Cianci's terms in office coincided with a dramatic physical transformation of downtown Providence. Given his considerable ego, it should surprise no one that Cianci claimed much of the credit for bringing about the city's revitalization.

Cianci spoke at urban planning seminars from Wilmington, Delaware, to San Diego. He attributed Providence's turnaround to [his] cheerleading and the city's strong-mayor form of government, which enabled him to cut through red tape and exert real leadership... (Stanton 2003, p. 228).

Providence's turnaround was somewhat more complicated than Cianci tended to suggest. Cianci liked to describe himself as a visionary, but he wasn't the architect or originator of the vision that transformed Providence. On the other hand, he was smart enough to recognize good ideas when they were presented to him, and, once having embraced them, worked tirelessly to bring them to fruition. In that regard, he was clearly fortunate to have had his thinking shaped by some remarkably capable and creative public servants in key city and state government departments, as well as by forward-looking leaders of the local business community, and visionary designers and planners such as William Warner and Marilyn Taylor.

Despite the unflattering media coverage Cianci often received, and the federal prosecutors' argument in their successful prosecution of Mayor Cianci that "the so-called Renaissance City was a city for sale," people I interviewed had remarkably positive things to say about the former mayor. Clark Schoettle, Executive Director of the Providence Revolving Fund, told me that "Cianci's art was to bring people together." People were especially appreciative of his strong and consistent support for historic preservation. "Buddy Cianci was one of the greatest preservationists in the city," declared Deming Sherman, Chairman of the Capital Center Commission. As part of its celebration of its 50th anniversary as an organization, the Providence Preservation Society honored Vincent Cianci in 2006 by inducting him into its Hall of Fame. Cianci was in federal prison at the time, and "sent his regrets, writing that he was figuratively and literally tied up" (Barry *ibid.*).

In *Providence: The Renaissance City*, Leazes and Motte state that "Cianci sought out useful allies" and worked "collaboratively … to establish a new policy direction for downtown (Leazes and Motte 2004, 66)." They also report he personally reached out to Antoinette Downing, the highly respected architectural historian, and sought her advice on how the city should use federal Community Development Block Grant (CDBG) funds that the mayor's office controlled.[17]

Vincent Cianci died in January 2016 at the age of 74, after falling ill while taping a television show. Joseph R. Paolino, Jr., whose own term in office as Providence's mayor was bookended by two of Cianci's administrations, was once a critic of Cianci. However, when informed of Cianci's death, Paolino issued a statement, saying, "Providence has lost its greatest champion. He gave his heart to Providence (*ibid.*)."

The Providence Foundation

By far one of the most important things that happened in Providence in the 1970s was the establishment of the Providence Foundation. The idea behind the Foundation was to create an entity composed of the presidents and CEOs of local corporations, banks and public utilities, which could exert a positive force in support of creative problem solving, and serve as a catalyst in bringing about beneficial projects and policy initiatives.[18] In the years that followed, the Foundation played a key role in helping advance a number of important revitalization initiatives.

One of the first initiatives spearheaded by the Providence Foundation was an effort to preserve and save the dilapidated Loews State Theater, the city's last remaining downtown theater, from being demolished. Ron Marsella, the Foundation's Executive Director at the time, recruited Robert Freeman, an architectural historian, to prepare the necessary documentation to nominate the theatre for listing on the National Register of Historic Places.[19] Having the theater listed on the National Register was especially important, because it was a pre-condition for the city to be able to use federal Community Development Block Grant funds toward the cost of renovation.

The renamed Ocean State Performing Arts Center reopened in October 1976: the first tangible evidence that progress was being made in reversing the decline of Downcity. In the 1990s, a city-wide campaign raised additional money to help pay for further capital improvements and interior renovations at the theater. Meanwhile, Mayor Cianci persuaded the City Council to approve the issuance of city bonds to pay for deepening the theater's stage to enable the theater to accommodate Broadway shows. The theater's stage was expanded in 1995, a state-of-the-art sound system was installed in 1996, and the theater's Arcade and Grand Lobby were restored in 1998. In 2005, the auditorium's seats were replaced and an elevator was installed that carries patrons between the Lobby and all other levels in the theater. The theater, now known as the Providence Performing Arts Center (PPAC), hasn't merely survived, but rather is thriving as never before, having become a popular venue for Broadway shows, concerts and a variety of other types of performances.

Chapter Five:

Northeast Railroad Corridor Relocation and Capital Center Project

In 1978, the federal government announced its intention to significantly upgrade the Northeast railroad corridor to bring about high-speed rail passenger service connecting Washington D.C., New York City, and Boston.[10] As part of that commitment, federal funding was earmarked to upgrade the rail corridor through Providence. At the time the announcement was made, it was assumed that the railroad tracks and station would remain where they were. However, fairly early on in the process, the idea of relocating the railroad tracks (first broached in the 1961 Downtown plan) re-surfaced.

Figure 5.1: Downtown Providence in February 1968: a "Chinese Wall" of elevated railroad tracks cut Downcity off from the State House, and the area in front of the State House is occupied by a sea of surface parking and jumble of roadways. (Source: The Providence Journal)

Sam Shamoon, the city's Associate Director of Planning, recalled that the track relocation idea was discussed at a meeting that involved the city's chief of planning (Martha Bailey), the chief of the planning division of the Rhode Island Department of Transportation (Joseph Arruda) and the executive director of the Providence Foundation (Ron Marsella). During that meeting, Robert Freeman, who years later would become executive director of the Providence Foundation, pulled out the 1961 Downtown plan and said, "Why don't we think about relocating the tracks? Maybe now is the time to do it."

Figure 5.2: View from train approaching downtown Providence from Boston, 1977.
(Source: Gene Bunnell)

Not long after that meeting, the Providence Foundation hired the firm of C. E. Maguire to evaluate the feasibility of relocating the tracks. The Maguire study concluded that the cost of relocating the railroad tracks was not much greater than the cost of completely reconstructing the existing track bed. Equally importantly, if not more so, it found that relocating the tracks would free up roughly 65 acres of land, which could then be redeveloped in a way that was economically beneficial to Amtrak, the State of Rhode Island, the P & W Railroad, and the City of Providence, all of which owned land in the area. Although the city owned the smallest share of the land, it stood to reap considerable economic benefit from the property taxes that would ultimately be generated by redeveloping such a large amount of underutilized land.

As a result of the findings of the Maguire study, Mayor Cianci became a strong supporter of the plan. State funding was obtained to hire the firm of Skidmore, Owings & Merrill LLP (SOM) to prepare a concept plan that would outline, in broad-brush terms, how the area might be reorganized and redeveloped once the tracks were relocated. SOM's Marilyn Taylor was in charge of this planning effort, which came to be called the "Capital Center project."

"Back then, the State House stood on top of a steep hill, and looked out onto freight yards that occupied the flat low-lying land at the base of the hill," said Shamoon (int.). The concept plan Taylor produced showed the railroad tracks being moved 600-850 feet to the north (toward the State House), and called for raising the elevation of the base of the hill to cover the tracks with a grassy lawn—thereby placing them out of view. Taylor's plan also called for introducing a major "water feature" that would create a strong radial axis between the State House and downtown, and provide a focal point for the low-lying area closest to the old Union Station.

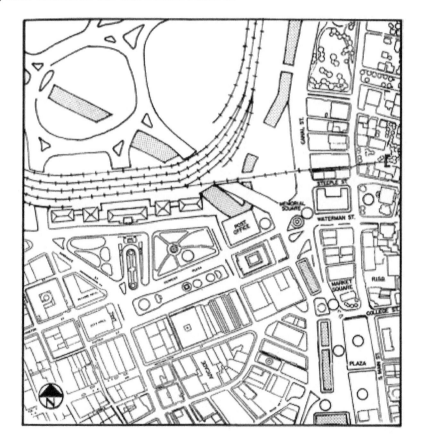

1980 SITE CONDITIONS

Figure 5.3: 1980 Capital Center Existing Conditions.

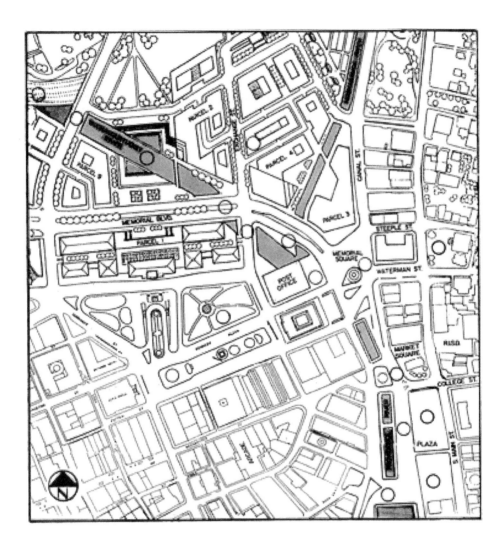

1981 CAPITAL CENTER PLAN

Figure 5.4: Original Capital Center Plan.

Meanwhile, attention shifted to securing the necessary governmental, regulatory and legislative approvals to implement the plan. The Federal Railroad Administration (FRA) approved the plan to move the railroad tracks and construct a new train station at Gaspee Street. The Federal Highway Administration (FHWA), the State of Rhode Island, and the City of Providence agreed to cooperate in constructing a new civic center interchange with I-95, as well as other connecting roads leading into the city. State legislation was passed establishing the Capital Center Special Development District, encompassing a total of 77 acres: an area somewhat larger that than the 65 acres C.E. Maguire initially identified as being potentially developable. State legislation was also passed establishing a 13-member Capital Center Commission (CCC), with the Governor, the mayor of Providence, and the chairman of the Providence Foundation each appointing four members, with the chairman of the commission jointly appointed by all three. The responsibilities outlined for the commission were to oversee the development process, and carry out a mandatory design review process related to all public and private development projects undertaken within the district.

Detailed "Design and Development Guidelines" were drafted and adopted by the commission, specifying what could and could not be built on the various parcels of land in the district: requirements that were in addition to what the pre-existing zoning required. When these guidelines were drafted and adopted, it was expected that most of the Capital Center land would be occupied by office buildings. Retail development was specifically prohibited on Capital Center land: a restriction put into place at the insistence of owners of downtown retail and department store properties, who feared competition.

One of the final regulatory hurdles that faced the Capital Center project was the need to carry out a federally mandated environmental impact study (EIS). Under federal law, impacts on historically and architecturally significant properties and resources need to be considered as well as impacts on the natural environment.

During the period leading up to the EIS, Antoinette Downing, the architectural historian and preservationist who played such an important role in the planning effort that saved and revitalized College Hill, seriously questioned whether the Capital Center project was a good idea. She particularly feared that commercial buildings developed on land freed up by relocating the railroad tracks would drain commercial activity and investment away from historic buildings in the city's traditional commercial core.

The EIS pertaining to the Capital Center project was carried out by Pete Pointner, who had previously worked for the firm of Delew Cather, but more recently had formed his own planning consulting firm called Planning Resources, Inc., in Wheaton, Illinois. The findings of Pointner's study helped allay Downing's concerns regarding the possible negative impact the Capital Center project might have on the downtown. In the study, Pointner calculated the expected rate at which new commercial space would be built, come on the market and be occupied, and concluded that the Capital Center project would not diminish interest in renovating and adaptively reusing historic buildings in downtown Providence. To the contrary: he concluded that the Capital Center project would serve as a "relief valve" that would *reduce* the pressure and temptation to tear down historic buildings in the center of the city.[20]

The method that was used to finance the Capital Center project, known as *land readjustment*, has not often been used in the U.S. Basically, land readjustment is a way of accomplishing the coordinated development of adjacent parcels of land owned by a number of different property owners. The advantage of this approach (as opposed to having a public redevelopment authority carry out the project by acquiring and consolidating the land by means of eminent domain) was that it was consensual, and avoided time-consuming and contentious condemnation proceedings.

As noted previously, four different entities owned portions of the land that was part of the Capital Center project: the City of Providence; the State of Rhode Island; Amtrak (i.e., the federal government); and Capital Properties, the real estate arm of Providence and Worcester Railroad. Of these four, Capital Properties owned by far the largest share of the land (see Figure 5.5). To carry out the project, the four parties entered into a contractual Memorandum of Agreement (MOA), under which they agreed to pool their land and work with one another in developing the land. Additionally, the parties designated the CCC to act on their behalf in carrying out the project, in accordance with the agreed-upon development plan, land use requirements, and design guidelines.

The overall project area was ultimately sub-divided into eleven parcels, each of which could be individually marketed and developed. To assure that the proportions of the land area owned by the respective property owners remained the same as at the beginning, a series of land swaps were undertaken between and among the property owners. Four additional parcels were later added to the project area, bringing the total number of parcels to fifteen.

Despite the many positive features of the initial Capital Center plan, it had a serious shortcoming in that it failed to address the traffic problems it would have created and worsened in adjoining parts of the downtown. Sam Shamoon at the city's Planning Department was one of the first to recognize that the highways and interchanges that were about to be built as part of the Capital Center project were going to channel a large amount of traffic into Memorial Square (aka "Suicide Circle"), and make traffic problems there much worse. Convinced that something needed to be done to alleviate the problem, he approached state highway officials and said, "You're bringing in a huge volume of traffic here. Where is it going to go?" The response he got was, essentially, "That's your job. You people at the city figure it out."

With the help of two members of his staff, Shamoon began to sketch out various ways that traffic coming into the Memorial Square area could be handled. The Memorial Square Committee was formed, which included the city traffic engineer and Ken Orenstein, executive director of the Providence Foun-

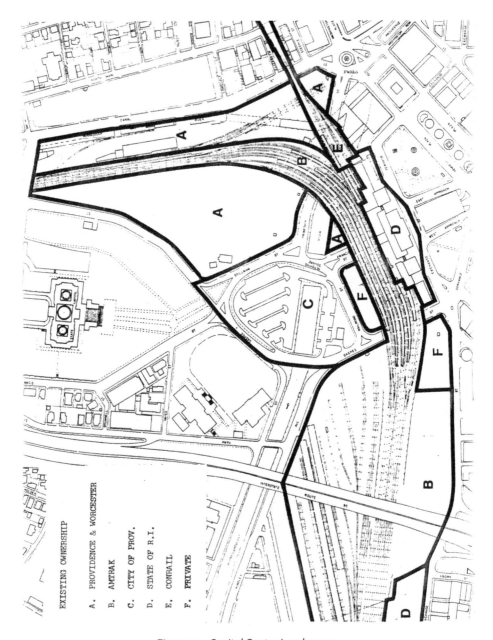

Figure 5.5: Capital Center Landowners
(Source: Union Station Relocation report, January 19, 1979)

dation. The firm of Wilbur Smith Associates was hired to carry out a detailed analysis. The analysis showed that the biggest factor contributing to congestion at Memorial Square was traffic funneling through the square to and from the east, through the College Hill area along Angell and Waterman Streets. By February 1983, Wilbur Smith Associates had come up with seven distinct traffic circulation alternatives for dealing with the problem, most of them calling for

Figure 5.6: Aerial photo of downtown Providence in October 1949. Memorial Square is in the center of the photo. To the right of Memorial Square is the post office, which was built over the Providence River. Above Memorial Square in the photo, an uncovered portion of the Providence River is visible, lined with parked cars. (Source: The Providence Journal)

extending Memorial Boulevard to the south. One of the alternatives called for extending Memorial Boulevard along the west side of the river, utilizing existing decking over the river in some places, and constructing additional decking over the river where necessary.[20] Around the same time, a new player appeared on the scene to urge a very different, much more daring approach.

Figure 5.7: Memorial Square (aka "Suicide Circle") in the 1980's
(Source: Providence Department of Planning and Development)

Uncovering and Relocating the Rivers

Architect/planner William D. Warner was no stranger to Providence, having previously worked for the Providence City Plan Commission as project director for the 1959 College Hill plan. In 1960, he opened a private architectural and planning firm in Providence, which later relocated to nearby Exeter. Warner nevertheless kept track of what was happening in Providence, and kept a close eye on the planning process that was underway related to Capital Center.

Warner was convinced that the city had made a serious mistake years ago when it had allowed the rivers that ran through the city to be almost completely decked over for parking. He also recognized that the city was about to undertake a major downtown project that was going to perpetuate the situation. Some people called it "the world's widest bridge;" it was really nine separate bridges, all interconnected. The tenth and final insult occurred in 1940 when the city's central post office was constructed over the entire width of the Providence River, just 40 feet south of its confluence.

As noted earlier, the original Capital Center plan prepared by SOM did not address the issue of the rivers, and kept them as they were: largely covered and out of sight. It also did not attempt to alleviate traffic problems that were going to arise at Memorial Square as a result of the project. With these issues in mind, Bill Warner went to see Bob Bendick, director of the Rhode Island Department of Environmental Management (RIDEM), to talk about taking a look at the larger picture of how highways were cutting the city off from its waterfront. The problem wasn't limited to the area near Memorial Square and the Capital Center District. I-195 cut the east side of the city off from the Narragansett Bay to the south; continuing west, I-195 crossed the Providence River at Old Harbor, leaving interchange ramps on both shores, from which service roads extended north to downtown.

Bendick agreed with Warner that a comprehensive planning study was needed to produce solutions that would restore the city's connection to its waterfront and minimize the negative impacts of highway traffic on the downtown. The timing seemed right for such a waterfront study. James Rouse, the nationally renowned developer of Faneuil Hall Marketplace in Boston and of Harborplace in Baltimore, had been brought to Providence in 1982, and was the keynote speaker at a conference organized by Brown University and *The Providence Journal* that focused on Providence's waterfront. Rouse's speech generated a great deal of publicity and enthusiasm for reclaiming Providence's waterfront. Rouse essentially said, "Look at what we're doing in Boston, and look at what we're doing in Baltimore. Everyone wants to be near the water. Go to the water!"

Bendick suggested that a possible source of funding for a waterfront study was the National Endowment for the Arts (NEA). Before going to work on preparing a funding application to NEA, Warner and Bendick went to discuss their ideas with Ed Wood, the newly appointed head of the Rhode Island Department of Transportation (RIDOT). Wood was an avid environmentalist, and had previously headed the Rhode Island Department of Environmental Management. "Warner's ideas fascinated Wood, and provided a way for the new RIDOT director to mollify his own reluctant feelings about taking the [RIDOT] post (Leazes and Motte 2004, 112)."

Warner completed the NEA grant application in the fall of 1982. He and Bendick then went to see Sam Shamoon, seeking the city's support for the NEA application. As reported by Leazes and Motte (*ibid.*) "there was such 'hemming and hawing' that both men left without approval having been given." Instead, they walked across the street to see Ken Orenstein at the Providence Foundation. Orenstein immediately expressed his support. The Providence Foundation agreed to sponsor the NEA grant application, as it had done for the *Interface* project in 1974, and to host the meetings that would be part of the planning process, and keep minutes. Governor Garrahy and Mayor Cianci came together to express their support for the waterfront revitalization study and the NEA grant application in February 1983.

On May 18, 1983, the NEA announced its grant award, which when added to the city, state and institutional money that had already been pledged, provided a total of $125,000 for the Providence Waterfront Study.[21] William Warner was engaged as director and designer of the study. In June, a 20-member Waterfront Study Coordinating Committee was established, composed of people from all over the city; representatives from all the state, federal and city agencies and departments that needed to be involved or had an interest in the project; and such private sector and nonprofit organizations as the Providence Preservation Society and Providence Foundation. Ken Orenstein, Executive Director of the Providence Foundation, chaired the committee.

The study was divided into three areas: the Providence River; Fox and India Point (the southern shoreline of the east side); and the Seekonk River (the eastern shoreline). Somewhat later, the Providence River was further subdivided into Old Harbor (the area south of the Crawford Street Bridge) and the segment north of the Crawford Street Bridge.

Because site preparation and construction of the underlying infrastructure was about to begin within the Capital Center project area, it was imperative that planning recommendations produced by the Waterfront Study be integrated with improvements planned for the Capital Center area. For that reason, the Providence Waterfront Study initially focused on the portion of the Providence River closest to the Capital Center project: the segment north of the Crawford Street Bridge.

Warner and the Waterfront Study were significantly constrained in their consideration of the design schemes by the looming Capital Center interchange. Sam Shamoon at the city's Planning Department analyzed a series of traffic alternatives, and drafted a memorandum for the city's Design Subcommittee for Memorial Square Traffic Alternatives, outlining how the city proposed to ease the traffic problems. According to Orenstein, what the Planning Department was proposing was, in essence, to widen roads and create additional decking over the rivers. Shamoon gave Ken Orenstein a copy of the memorandum prior to the meeting of the Subcommittee. Orenstein was "aghast" that the city was proposing to further pave over the rivers. As reported by Leazes and Motte:

> Orenstein, hoping to forestall what he viewed as a grave mistake
> by the city, showed the plans to Warner on Sunday, 21 February

1983 [one day before the Design Subcommittee was scheduled to meet to review the traffic alternatives] at Warner's Exeter, Rhode Island home. He urged Warner to do something, anything to stop the plans from going forward (Leazes and Motte 2004, 114).

Warner and his wife sketched out a number of schematics in response to this plea to "do something." Warner also pulled out and revisited year-old doodles, which he had drawn on napkins, in which he'd played with various design ideas. Warner had long believed that a series of bridges, with open water in between them, would improve traffic flow and beautify the area. At this early stage in his thinking, "adding bridges and extending Memorial Boulevard south toward the waterfront were at the core of his plan, not moving rivers (*ibid.*, 114).

Warner gave his sketches to Orenstein, who presented them to the Memorial Square Design Subcommittee's February 22, 1983 meeting. RIDOT's Ed Wood and DEM's Bob Bendick supported Warner's design ideas because they were opposed to more decking. Ron Marsella was somewhat more circumspect and suggested that Warner present his ideas to the Capital Center Commission.

The members of the Waterfront Study Coordinating Committee met twice monthly between June and October 1983. At one of those meetings (July 1983), Warner unveiled a seemingly radical scheme that raised the possibility of *relocating the rivers*. At first, the idea of moving the rivers seemed crazy and totally impractical. However, the more people thought about it, the more the idea seemed worth considering. The "River Relocation" scheme Warner developed called for moving the river out from under the post office and relocating the confluence of the rivers nearly 100 yards to the east. It would then be possible to construct an extension of Memorial Boulevard on solid ground between the post office and the rivers' new confluence and, most importantly, *to uncover the rivers*.

Between July and October 1983, the members of the Waterfront Study Coordinating Committee worked together to overcome potential obstacles and refine the plan. In August 1983, after a lengthy discussion, the committee agreed that the city should amend Wilbur Smith's Memorial Square/Crawford Street design contract to have them look at the traffic implications of the Providence Waterfront Study. They also discussed the importance of trying to keep the Capital Center project "on track ... without closing the door to the ideas being developed by the Providence Waterfront Study." According to the minutes of that August meeting, Joseph Arruda, who headed the planning

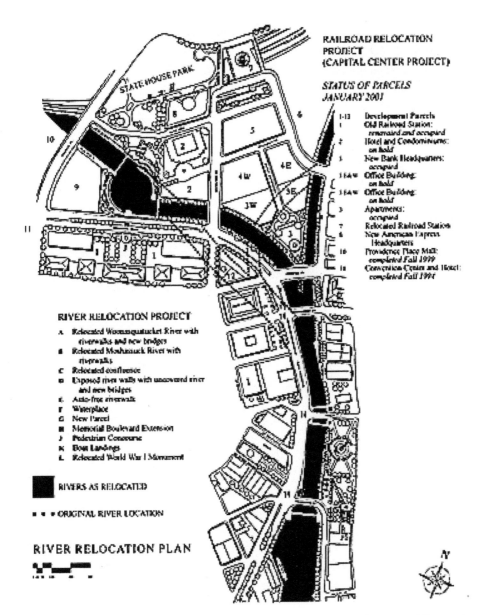

Figure 5.8: 1983 River Relocation Plan (Source: William D. Warner, Architects and Planners)

division of RIDOT, commented that if the Memorial Boulevard Extension could be classified as an "urban connector" highway, it would be eligible for 85% federal funding. "That was the real breakthrough in thinking about how we could implement and pay for this more ambitious downtown plan," said Shamoon (int.).

By October, the final version of the Memorial Boulevard Extension/River Relocation plan had taken shape and been endorsed by the committee. A little later in the fall of 1983, as construction work on the Capital Center project was about to begin, RIDOT agreed to "pull" the Memorial Boulevard Extension/

River Relocation part of the Providence Waterfront Study for the purpose of conducting an Environmental Impact Statement (EIS) on the project: an action that was intended to advance the project closer to the implementation stage, so that it could, it was hoped, be coordinated with the Capital Center project.

Upon learning about the recommendations contained in the Providence Waterfront Study, and the possibility that the rivers through downtown might be relocated, Ron Marsella started making telephone calls. Marsella had previously served as executive director of the Providence Foundation but had left that position to become a private developer, and was about to develop a major downtown office building right where Warner's plan called for relocating a river. Marsella was understandably upset by the prospect that his development project might have to be delayed by this "pie-in-the-sky" idea of relocating the rivers through downtown. Sam Shamoon recalls Marsella angrily saying, "This idea of relocating the rivers is going to stop me in my tracks. I can't let that happen. I bet any amount of money this project will never happen!"

For a while, the politics surrounding the project became pretty sticky. Marsella was well known and highly respected in the Providence business community. He also knew many people in important positions. Moreover, the city did not want to lose the substantial investment Marsella was promising to make in downtown. Marsella did have a point: moving rivers is not a simple matter and raises serious environmental issues. A detailed EIS would have to be prepared and permits from environmental agencies would need to be obtained.

Around this time, Pete Pointner, who had conducted the EIS on the Capital Center project, received a call from a developer in Providence, whose name he has not revealed. According to Pointner, the telephone conversation went like this: "The developer began by asking me, 'What do you think of a project involving moving rivers in a downtown?' I said, 'Well, on the surface, it sounds like it would be impossible to obtain the permits.' It sounded to me at the time like some crazy scheme cooked up by a developer who was intent on screwing the environment to get more building space" (Pointner int.). The last thing the developer said to Pointner as their telephone conversation ended was, "If you don't bring us together and help us resolve this conflict, we're in trouble" (*ibid.*).

Pointner was hired and brought back to Providence to assess the environmental issues raised by the proposed river relocation, and to work with Warner and Wilbur Smith Associates on the preparation of a detailed EIS. The EIS evaluated and compared a number of traffic alternatives, including the alternative that called for uncovering and relocating the rivers and placing the proposed Memorial Boulevard Extension along the west side of the river.

The EIS was completed in six months and selected the River Relocation plan as the preferred alternative. In August 1984, a formal public hearing was held, at which almost all the comments regarding the River Relocation/Memorial Boulevard Extension project were strongly in favor. In November of that year, the city, the state, and the FHWA committed to the project's funding. Because of the collaborative nature of the planning process, and the favorable response the plan received at the public hearing, only minor amendments were required and all necessary environmental clearances were obtained not long thereafter.

In February 1985, Warner and C. E. Maguire (engineers for the Capital Center project) began preparing detailed design and engineering plans for the Memorial Boulevard Extension/River Relocation project. In the fall of 1987, four years after construction began on the Capital Center project, the complicated task of reclaiming the city's waterfront by uncovering and relocating the rivers began.

Owing to the River Relocation Project, the office building Ron Marsella had wanted to build in the mid-1980s didn't get built until 1990. In retrospect, Marsella was probably fortunate he wasn't able to build his building when and where he wanted. Had the building not been delayed, it would have come on the market around the time of the 1987-88 real estate market collapse, when there was a glut of vacant new office buildings throughout New England. The unique qualities of the new site also conferred considerable prestige on the building. The three-sided, thirteen-story building that ended up being built at the relocated confluence of Moshassuck and Woonasquatucket Rivers, designed by Jung-Brannen Architects of Boston, is unquestionably one of the most readily recognized and admired buildings in Providence.

Between 1981 and 1985, the Capital Center design plan was refined and modified, taking account of the area wide changes brought about by the River Relocation and Memorial projects. The "water feature" Marilyn Taylor initially envisioned evolved into the circular body of water known today as Waterplace Cove, which makes an obvious historic reference to the shallow cove that existed in the 19th century, before it was filled in with soil removed from Weybosset Hill. Taylor's design scheme for Waterplace Park also included a 30-foot high fountain, an amphitheater, several smaller plazas with seating, two pedestrian bridges and a pavilion.

A wide, arched underpass underneath Memorial Boulevard, positioned between the former Union Station building and the (Marriott) Courtyard Providence Downtown on Memorial Boulevard, provides pedestrian access to Waterplace Park from Burnside Park and Kennedy Place. At the opposite end of the Waterplace Cove, a ceremonial staircase provides a visually dramatic way to

Figure 5.9: In this photograph taken in 1994, decking has been largely removed from over the Providence River, and construction of Memorial Blvd. Extension has begun. (Source: William D. Warner, Architects and Planners)

Figure 5.10: Completed Memorial Boulevard Extension/River Relocation Project, as viewed from the Citizens Plaza office building. Note the wide riverside public plaza and promenade on the left alongside buildings of the Rhode Island School of Design, and the relocated World War I Memorial in Memorial Park. (Source: Department of Planning and Development, City of Providence)

Figure 5.11: Citizens Plaza office building at the relocated confluence of rivers.
(Source: Gene Bunnell)

approach the Rhode Island State House. Each succeeding step up the staircase reveals more and more of the State House. At the top of the staircase, one looks out across an expansive grassy area. There are no trees in this area to impede the view because the soil here is fairly shallow—the reason being that the lawn covers tunnels through which trains pass in and out of Providence's railroad station. Looking more closely, one can see a number of low-rise structures that may look somewhat like planting beds, but which are vents that have been put in place over the tunnels to vent fumes generated by diesel locomotives.

Over 11 acres of riverfront parks were created as a combined result of the Capital Center, River Relocation and Memorial Boulevard Extension projects, the largest and most prominent being Waterplace Park (4 acres); Memorial Park (2 acres), now the home of the World War I monument formerly located at Memorial Square, was doubled in size.[22]

A number of smaller public spaces and plazas were also introduced at other points along the riverwalks. One such inviting public space overlooking the Providence River is set against the backdrop of buildings that are part of the campus of the Rhode Island School of Design. Anticipating the positive effect that the River Relocation project was going to have on its riverside location, RISD assembled and now controls an eclectic collection of buildings extending the entire block overlooking the river.

Figure 5.12: Waterplace Park and the ceremonial staircase leading up from Waterplace Cove toward the State Housel, as viewed from the Marriott Courtyard Hotel. (Source: Gene Bunnell)

Figure 5.13: The low-rise structures in this photograph, which look somewhat like planting beds, vent fumes from the railroad tunnels that pass under this grassy area across the street from Providence Place mall. (Source: Gene Bunnell)

Figure 5.14: Waterplace Cove as viewed from Francis Street in front of Providence Place mall. The archway opening in the center of the picture is the pedestrian underpass which provides access to Waterplace Park from offices and restaurants in the old Union Station complex as well as from Burnside Park and Kennedy Plaza. (Source: Gene Bunnell)

Figure 5.15: Memorial Park and the relocated World War I Memorial, with the Providence County Courthouse in the background. (Source: Gene Bunnell)

Figure 5.16: Riverside public space adjoining a row of buildings associated with Rhode Island School of Design. (Source: Gene Bunnell)

An Exceptional Setting for *Waterfire*

As part of the River Relocation/Memorial Boulevard Extension projects, the rivers through downtown Providence were dredged. In addition, all the bridges constructed over the rivers were built with clearances more than adequate to allow for the passage of small boats underneath them. Boats can now navigate to and from Waterplace Cove, utilizing nearly a mile of downtown river channels. This outcome might not have been much appreciated at the outset, but it certainly is now owing to the enormous popularity of *Waterfire,* a unique and entrancing public art installation which attracts tens of thousands of people to downtown Providence throughout the summer and fall. Without these river-related improvements and design features, it is fair to say that installing and staging *Waterfire* would not have been operationally feasible.

Barnaby Evans, the creator of Waterfire, has worked in many media, including site-specific sculpture installations, photography, garden design, architectural projects, film, writing and conceptual works.[23] Originally trained in the sciences, Evans received his Sc.B. degree in biology and environmental science from Brown University in 1975. Evans' first installation of *Waterfire* in Providence took place in 1994. This initial installation proved so popular that a second installation of Waterfire ("Second Fire") was staged in June 1996. In that same year, a non-profit 501(c)(3) organization was established, called "Waterfire Providence", to carry on and make possible a continuation of annual installations of *Waterfire.* Since then, *Waterfire* has been staged on numerous occasions each year, aided by hundreds of volunteers and financial contributions from throughout the community.

Waterfire is more than just an installation of public art. It has also produced significant economic development benefits for the city and state. *Waterfire* attracts about 1.1 million people to Providence each year, generating $114.3 million in visitor spending and $9.3 million in tax revenue for the State of Rhode Island and City of Providence, and creating 1,294 jobs for local residents.[24] A survey of 4,248 people who attended *Waterfire* in 2004 found that 57% traveled to Providence from out of state to see the event.

A few summers ago, my wife and I traveled to Providence to experience *Waterfire.* We arrived around 5:00 PM, and found a rare parking space on College Hill behind a museum. We strolled through the College Hill neighborhood for a while, and then walked down College Street to the Providence River. Families with children and people of all ages had already staked out places to sit with good views of the water. By 8:00 PM, thousands of people filled the full length of the riverwalks along both sides of the river.

A long line of steel braziers holding stacks of firewood had been placed down

Figure 5.17: View looking down from top flow of the 28-story Sovereign Bank office building, showing the relocated confluence of rivers, the nearby College Hill neighborhood and historic First Baptist Church (1774-1775). Roger Williams National Park is visible just above and to the right of the triangular Citizens Plaza building. (Source: Gene Bunnell)

Figure 5.18: Volunteers loading wood into braziers in the middle of the Providence River in preparation for *Waterfire*. (Source: Gene Bunnell)

the centerline of the river, and also in a circle around the perimeter of Waterplace Cove. As darkness fell, people dressed in black capes standing in black boats began floating slowly and quietly up the canal, lighting the stacks of wood. Eventually all the braziers were alight. Mysterious and eerie sounds seemed to be emanating from within the water. According to Waterfire Providence's website, the music that accompanies *Waterfire* is an integral component of the installation.[25]

Figure 5.19: Display of Waterfire on a summer night in Providence, viewed looking across Waterplace Cove toward buildings in Downcity. (Source: Michael Melford, Providence Tourism Council)

Throughout the evening, black barges loaded with more firewood moved slowly and silently back and forth through the water, repeatedly replenishing the wood in the braziers to keep the fires burning. The air was filled with the aromatic scent of the specially selected mixture of firewood that is used for *Waterfire*. Three different kinds of wood are reportedly used in *Waterfire*, each one selected to contribute to a different sensation—light, smell, and heat. Sparks shot into the air like sparklers on the Fourth of July, then spiraled down into the water that reflected the intense glow of the fires.

The combination of sensations—the intense heat and light of the fires, the reflected glow of flames dancing on the water, the arresting scent of the wood, and the mysterious background music—was mezmerizing. Consider the extraordinariness of what we witnessed. Thousands of people had come to sit quietly and watch wood burn: not something that one would normally draw a huge crowd. Then again, people weren't just watching wood burn. What made the experience of *Waterfire* special was the setting within which the event took place.

How many of the people who were in attendance that evening knew what the area looked like not so long ago? How many knew how the walkways and public spaces along the rivers that provided such a wonderful setting for viewing *Waterfire* came to be? One reason for writing this book is so that more people will know.

Chapter Six:

Developing Capital Center

The first Capital Center development projects to be completed involved the renovation and conversion of the former Union Station into office and restaurant space. The Rhode Island Foundation, the Providence Foundation, and Greater Providence Chamber of Commerce occupied the upper floor office space, and the Union Station Brewery and Capital Grill occupied floor space on the lower level. Another early Capital Center project involved construction of a new railroad station for Amtrak, which opened in 1987, along with a 360-car underground parking garage.

Figure 6.1: Former Union Railroad Station, now an office building. (Source: Gene Bunnell)

Figure 6.2: "New" Railroad Station constructed in 1987. (Source: Gene Bunnell)

Variety of Land Uses Accommodated

When the Capital Center project was initially planned, it was generally expected that most of the cleared land within the project area would be occupied by office buildings. The first office building built at Capital Center was completed in 1989, and was initially occupied by American Express. The second office building, completed in 1990, was the architecturally striking 13-story Citizens Plaza office building developed by Ron Marsella at the relocated confluence of the two rivers. For many years thereafter, however, no additional office building projects were built. It wasn't until 2006, sixteen years after the Citizens Plaza building was completed, that a third office building was developed, the 210,000 sq. ft. headquarters of GTECH that makes lottery tickets and equipment used by state lotteries.[26] A fourth 325,000 sq. ft. office building was completed in 2010 to serve as the headquarters of Blue Cross/ Blue Shield of Rhode Island.

Little thought appears to have been given at the outset to the possibility that Capital Center land might accommodate housing. Such an oversight is somewhat understandable, given the fact that the city's population was declining back in the 1980s when the Capital Center project was being planned. Also, few people at the time fully appreciated the transformative effect the River Relocation/Memorial Boulevard Extension projects were going to have, and the extent to which they were going to make adjoining areas appealing as places to live.

Figure 6.3: GTECH headquarters office building (Source: Gene Bunnell)

The first residential development to take place within Capital Center was Avalon at Center Place, an 8-story, 225-unit project completed in 1990, built a short distance away from the "new" railroad station. The Avalon at Center Place project, located at 50 Park Row West, also included 350 underground structured parking spaces. More than a decade elapsed before a second residential development project was undertaken on Capital Center land: a 193-unit high-rise condominium development with 475 underground parking spaces, called Waterplace. The developers of this project had initially planned to sell the units as condominiums, but the project's completion coincided with the 2006-2008 financial crisis. Unable to sell the units as condominiums, the units were offered for rent. Today the development is fully occupied.

The most recent residential development within the Capital Center was built along the Moshassuck River, across the river from the Roger Williams National Park. A second apartment building, approved by the Capital Center Commission, will extend residential development further north along the Moshassuck River.

As noted earlier, retail development was initially prohibited from taking place on Capital Center land: a restriction that remained in place for many years. After the last downtown department store closed in the 1980s, however, and there was hardly any downtown retail activity left to protect, the prohibition against retail development was lifted, clearing the way for the eventual development of Providence Place mall.

Figure 6.4: Avalon at Center Place apartment complex overlooking downtown Providence and the Riverwalk along the Woonasquatucket River. The massive granite blocks that line the Riverwalk, and were used to channel the relocated river, came from the "Chinese Wall" that formerly supported the elevated railroad tracks that that ran through downtown Providence. (Source: Gene Bunnell)

Figure 6.5: View from the Biltmore Hotel's 16th floor ballroom, that shows the Waterplace residential development project in relation to Waterplace Park, the State House and Providence Place Mall. (Source Gene Bunnell)

Figure 6.6: Waterplace apartment complex overlooking Waterplace Cove. The project's proximity to Waterplace Park adds to the appeal as a place to live. (Source: Gene Bunnell)

Figure 6.7: Apartment development on Capital Center land along the Moshassuck River. (Source: Gene Bunnell)

Providence Convention Center

Although the Providence Convention Center was built outside the boundaries of the Capital District project area, it nonetheless had a significant influence on the development that subsequently took place within Capital Center. By developing a convention center connected to a major hotel, a new policy objective had implicitly been established for Providence and for Capital Center: that of making Providence a "destination city (Leazes and Motte 2004, 177-178)".

The idea of developing a downtown convention center had been around since the 1950s, but had been continually postponed due to a lack of public financing. By the mid-1980s, however, Rhode Island's economy had entered a period of relative prosperity, and "the state [was] awash in revenues (Leazes and Motte 2004, 166)." Meanwhile, the rivers were about to be moved as part of carrying out the ambitious Memorial Boulevard Extension project, further contributing to the sense that it was time for the state to take decisive action in spearheading the revitalization of the state's capital city.

In 1987, the Rhode Island General Assembly passed legislation creating the Rhode Island Convention Center Authority (RICCA). The legislation granted RICCA the power to issue bonds to acquire land and to construct, manage and operate a downtown convention center.

A new hotel adjacent and connected to the convention center was recognized as essential to a successful convention center; consequently, building a convention center hotel became an implicit element of RICCA's mission. In 1988, the authority secured a $42 million loan to buy the Bonanza Bus station, two parking lots, and other state properties; in spring 1990 it secured private financing for a hotel (*ibid.*, 167).

In November 1990 Buddy Cianci was re-elected as Mayor, after six years out of office. Shortly after being inaugurated in January 1991, Cianci cancelled the agreement entered into by the city's previous mayor, Joseph Paolino, thereby withdrawing the city's pledge of financial support for the operating costs of the convention center.

With the convention center project unraveling, the state's recently elected Governor, Bruce Sundlun, made a public plea for the project in April 1991, arguing that the convention center was critical to the future of Providence and Rhode Island as a whole (*ibid.*, 169). RICCA chair Richard Oster supported the Governor's position, citing findings of feasibility and marketing studies that showed that a downtown convention center would generate significant economic activity and revenue. Based on those forecasts, the authority moved ahead with the project without city assistance.

RICCA had hoped to find a private firm willing to pay for and operate a hotel, and actively sought bidders, but without success. Rather than jeopardize the economic viability of the convention center by opening it without an adjacent hotel, the authority made use of its legislatively granted authority to issue state revenue bonds to finance the construction of a 261-room hotel, which was initially operated by the Westin Hotel chain. RICCA also made use of state-issued revenue bonds to finance the construction of two associated parking garages.[27]

Providence Place Mall

The vast majority of shopping malls that have been developed in this country have been built in outlying, suburban areas, where assembling large tracts of vacant land is fairly easy. Surrounded by acres of surface parking, such freestanding shopping malls have little need to "fit in" to their surroundings. Developing a 1.5 million sq. ft. shopping mall in the center of Providence required a good deal more forethought and sophistication.

Figure 6.8: 1992 aerial photo of downtown Providence. The railroad tracks have been relocated, and the Moshassuck and Woonasquatucket Rivers have also been relocated. A new railroad station and four major buildings have been constructed on various development parcels within Capital Center. The site on which the Providence Place mall will later be built is the surface parking lot visible in the top center of this photo. (Source: William D. Warner, Architects and Planners)

Assembling the land necessary to construct the mall presented significant challenges, requiring multi-party negotiations and agreements involving state government, the city, agencies of the federal government (such as Amtrak), and the developers. The developers needed to acquire four and a half acres of land owned by Amtrak, and seven acres from the state. The Providence City Council also needed to vote to approve enlarging the boundaries of the Capital Center District to incorporate the previously referenced seven acres of state land within the boundaries of the Capital Center District. Last but not least, the CCC needed to drop the prohibition of retail development within the Capital District.

All of the above actions were accomplished. However, further progress in moving the project forward was brought to a halt by the Rhode Island Credit Union crisis of 1989-1994. In the years leading up to 1989, residential home prices had increased dramatically in Rhode Island, contributing to rampant speculation in real estate, and leading credit unions and small banks in the state to over-extend themselves in lending money for large-scale residential developments. When the housing bubble burst, local banks and credit unions began to fail.

Between 1990 and 1993, financing for almost any kind of real estate development in Rhode Island was essentially unavailable. During this hiatus, the development team that had begun the process of attempting to build the mall was replaced by a new team, led by Pyramid Corporation. Major retail tenants still needed to be found to anchor the mall. In 1993, Mayor Cianci, Governor Sundlun, and Joseph Paolino traveled to Seattle, along with Robert Congrell (the head of Pyramid Corporation), to try to sell the Nordstrom family on the idea of locating a Nordstrom department store in the mall they hoped would be built in Providence (*ibid.*, 163).

By 1993, it had become evident that for the mall to be built in a workable manner, the nearby building that housed the University of Rhode Island's College of Continuing Education (URI-CCE) would have to be demolished. Finding a suitable new home for URI-CCE became a priority. The solution that was arrived at was to renovate the former Shepard's Department Store building on Westminster Street, which had stood vacant for two decades. URI-CCE was relocated to that building: which not only met the needs of the college but also generated activity beneficial to downtown.

The most controversial issue related to the proposed mall was how to pay for the parking garage needed by the mall. The mall's developers insisted that without a public financial commitment to build the garage, there could be no Providence Place mall. But with the state of Rhode Island in the midst of a budget crisis due to plummeting tax receipts caused by the statewide reces-

Figure 6.9: Former Shepard's Department Store on Westminster Street, now the University of Rhode Island's College of Continuing Education. (Source: Gene Bunnell)

sion, direct state funding of the garage was out of the question. Nor could the City of Providence afford to take on that financial burden.

Further complicating the matter was the widespread perception that people going to a shopping mall would not be willing to pay for parking—and that if they did have to pay for parking, they wouldn't go there to shop. In the end, "a single purpose taxing district was created, and sales tax revenue generated by the mall was dedicated to pay off the bonds issued by the state to finance the construction of the garage (Orenstein 2015, personal communication)."[28]

Design and Appearance of Providence Place Mall

Concerns regarding the design and appearance of the proposed Providence Place mall represented the last hurdle to be overcome for the project to secure the approval of Capital Center Commission. "Design was a critical issue throughout the process of building the mall, and one that was central to preservationists' support for the project. Since the College Hill rescue of the 1950s, historic preservation remained a powerful urban policy concern (Leazes and Motte 2004, 153)." Implicit in these concerns was an insistence that the design of the mall be context-sensitive and respectful of its surroundings.

Concerns regarding the massing and design of the proposed mall were made all the more pressing by its prominent, highly visible location. As the PPS's Executive Director said at the time, the proposed Providence Place mall came "very close to putting a shopping mall on the State House lawn (as quoted by Leazes and Motte 2004, 155)." State Historic Preservation Officer Frederick Williamson at the Rhode Island Historical Preservation Commission observed that the way shopping malls were typically designed was very much at odds with the fabric of an old city and state capital like Providence.

> The architecture frequently used for such buildings involves large volumes of interior space with little exterior articulation in the form of frequent entrances, storefronts, window fenestration and variations in mass… Such buildings could be a visual intrusion on surrounding historic properties and therefore constitute an adverse effect (as quoted by Leazes and Motte, *ibid.*).

What Williamson feared turned out to be the case. The initial design of Providence Place submitted to the Capital Center Commission's Design Review Committee was a typical mall, with no storefronts. Moreover, Nordstrom's, a major anchor tenant of the mall, insisted that there be no outside doors leading into their store.

Most shopping malls are designed by a single architectural design firm. In the case of Providence Place mall, three different teams of architects and designers were involved. Macy's had their own architect for their end of the

Figure 6.10: Providence Place mall. (Source: Gene Bunnell)

mall; Nordstrom had their own architects for their end of the mall; a separate team of architects designed the central portion (Sherman int.).

The CCC employed its own team of architects to review and critique the design plans of the other three teams of architects. One of the architects brought in by the CCC to review the design and work with the mall architects and modify the plan was Friedrich St. Florian, a RISD faculty member. As a result of St.Florian's efforts, a glass façade was added to the central portion of the mall looking out onto Waterplace Park. "We [the CCC] spent two years reviewing the design of the project," said Sherman. The goal was to make the mall look like three separate buildings, rather than one single massive box, so as to resemble somewhat a classic New England mill complex" (Sherman int.).

Positive Synergies of the Convention Center, Convention Center Hotel and Providence Place

In 1994, the Providence Convention Center was completed, along with its associated hotel (initially a Westin Hotel; now an Omni Hotel). Five years later in 1999, Providence Place mall opened. The combination of the Convention Center and hotel proved so successful that in 2007 the convention center hotel was expanded by constructing a second tower containing 200 additional hotel rooms, 103 residential condominiums, 11,000 sq. ft. of ground floor retail space and 160 structured parking spaces. Because this second tower, like the first, was built on land within the Capital Center district, it also went through the CCC's rigorous design review process.

All three major downtown activity generators (the convention center, the hotel and Providence Place) are connected (see Figures 6.12 and 6.13). The convention center spans West Exchange Street and connects with the second floor corridor in the hotel where "break-out" rooms are located. There is also a walkway connecting the hotel to the convention center that spans Memorial Boulevard, as well as a physical connection between the hotel and the mall. "So it is possible to walk indoors above street level from the mall to the hotel and from there to the convention center" (Orenstein, 2015 int.).

All three major downtown destinations, including the mall, appear to be doing well economically. "J.C. Penny has downsized, but Macy's and Nordstrom are doing fine. The mall just landed a Spanish retailer, Zaro, which is helping keep it fresh. Eight to ten million people shop at the mall annually" (Baudouin int.).

As noted earlier, it had been feared that if people had to pay for parking they would not shop at the mall. However, this has not proven to be the case. "From the mall's opening until a couple of years ago the charge for parking was

Figure 6.11: Second tower added to convention center hotel in 2007. (Source: Gene Bunnell)

$1.00 for up to three hours, with the cost rising significantly for longer stays. A few years ago, the fee was increased to $2.00 for up to three hours. Many visitors to other downtown attractions park at the mall because it is significantly cheaper than metered, on-street parking spaces, most of which limit parking to two hours" (Motte, 2015 personal communication).

Direct and Indirect Impacts of the Capital Center Project

Not long after the Convention Center and Providence Place opened, additional hotels were developed within the Capital Center project area. A 215-room Marriott Courtyard hotel opened in 2000, on a portion of the land formerly occupied by the old Union Station. In point of fact, the Courtyard Providence Downtown occupies that portion of the former Union Station property that had been occupied by the tracks and station platforms prior to the rail corridor's relocation. The design of the hotel is a fine example of con-

Figure 6.12: 2004 aerial photo of the Capital Center project area, showing Providence Place mall, the convention center hotel and convention center) fronting on Francis Street (left side of photo). Note also how the Woonasquatucket River passes underneath and through Providence Place mall. (Source: the Capital Center Commission)

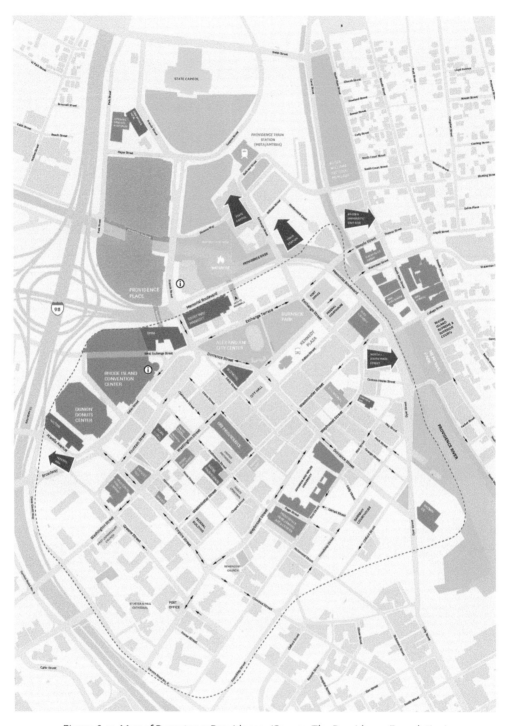

Figure 6.13: Map of Downtown Providence. (Source: The Providence Foundation)

text-sensitive architecture. The color and texture of brick used for its exterior makes it appear as if it were part of the original Union Station from the beginning. The hotel also includes a 300-space parking garage.

A few years after the Marriott Courtyard opened, an even more remarkable hotel project was undertaken: the construction of a 274-room Renaissance Hotel within the walls of the long-abandoned former Masonic Temple on Francis Street. Construction of the Masonic Temple began in 1928, but was never completed because of the stock market crash of 1929. For 75 years, the building stood vacant, and steadily deteriorated. By the time a plan for utilizing the structure was finalized, the interior of the building had deteriorated so badly it was necessary to completely gut the building, and build an entirely new structure within the Masonic Temple's outer walls.

The Renaissance Hotel, located directly across the street from the Rhode Island State House, opened in 2007. The total cost of the project, which qualified for federal and state historic preservation tax credits, was $81,500,000.

Additional hotels have been developed outside, but not far from, the Capital Center project area—further evidence of Providence's growing appeal as a visitor destination. None of these new downtown hotels has involved new construction; rather, they have been brought about by restoring and repurposing old buildings, such as the Hotel Providence on Mathewson Street, and a former office building on Weybosset Street, which was converted into a Hampton Inn. One of the most notable downtown hotel projects involved the conversion of a building on Fountain Street (circa 1912) that for decades housed the "Sportsman's Inn," a notorious strip-club and brothel. The building is now a 52-room boutique hotel, called The Dean.

The total amount of development and investment that has taken place within the boundaries of the Capital Center is impressive. As of 2015, the totals were as follows:

- $1.1 billion in private investment;

- $1.5 billion in combined public and private investment;

- One million square feet of office space;

- 1000 new residential units;

- 1,500 hotel rooms;

- 1,500,000 sq. ft. of new retail space;

- 10,000 structured parking spaces.

Figure 6.14: Outer walls of former Masonic Temple after the building's interior was removed. (Source: Clark Schoettle, Providence Revolving Fund)

Figure 6.15:New hotel constructed within outer walls of former Masonic Temple. (Source: Clark Schoettle, Providence Revolving Fund)

Figure 6.16: Renaissance Hotel in 2016 as viewed from the State House lawn
(Source: Gene Bunnell)

Figure 6.17: The Dean Hotel. (Source: Gene Bunnell)

In most old American cities, redeveloping downtown areas has required clearing away existing buildings and uprooting long established businesses and residents—typically with dire consequences for those residents and businesses. What makes the Capital Center project so remarkable is that it was carried out with almost no demolition or displacement. The one exception was the need to relocate the University of Rhode Island's College of Continuing Education to the former Shepard's Department Store building on Westminster Street—a move which benefited both the college and the city's downtown.

Capital Center Controversy Concerning Surface Parking

Prior to the Capital Center project, a large amount of the area in front of the Rhode Island State House was used for surface parking (See again Figure 5.1). The aim of the Capital Center plan was to intensively develop this potentially valuable land in ways that would be economically beneficial to the owners of the land, as well as enhance the image and attractiveness of downtown Providence. Implicit in that purpose was a recognition that surface parking was an inefficient way to use such centrally located land, and should be discouraged. Over 3000 parking spaces were eliminated when the Capital Center project went ahead.

The state legislation that created the CCC required any development project that took place within the boundaries of the Capital Center to secure the approval of the commission. The legislation also required the commission to develop a specific set of land use and design guidelines (which were adopted by the commission in 1989), and required that developments within the project area comply with those guidelines. Among other things, the land use and design guidelines that were adopted required that parking be provided either in parking structures or underground. As of 2015, 10,000 structured parking spaces had been developed within Capital Center.

Over time, the amount of the Capital Center land devoted to surface parking has been dramatically reduced—the most notable remaining area of surface parking as of 2016 being in the vicinity of the Citizen's Bank building. According to the Capital Center Commission's chairman: "The parking around the Citizens Bank building is 'temporary.' These lots are intended for development, and will hopefully be built on some day" (Sherman, 2015 personal communication). To make sure that this surface parking remains temporary, the land it occupies is leased for one year at a time. "Each year the property owner has to go back to the commission to get an extension of the land lease" (Orenstein, personal communication).

Given this history, it came as quite a surprise when the CCC's authority to prohibit surface parking was challenged by none other than the State of Rhode Island. This unexpected turn of events unfolded in 2012 when the State sought approval for the construction of surface parking at the expense of part of the State House lawn: a clear violation of Capital Center regulations. A compromise was worked out when the proposed design of the parking lot was modified to retain some trees. "Despite the agreement, the State still wanted to seek a waiver contesting the Capital Center Commission's right to oversee the design, and the project was put on hold (Fain, WPRI.com, 2013)."

Three years later, the State resubmitted its plans for a surface parking lot to the CCC "as a courtesy," but remained unwilling to acknowledge the commission's jurisdiction. "The irony," noted CCC chairman Deming Sherman, "is that the State was one of the original signatories to the documents that created the commission in the first place" (*ibid.*).

As noted previously, the land that was used for the Capital Center project was owned by four different parties. Of those, Capital Properties, the real estate arm of Providence & Worcester Railroad, owned by far the largest amount of land. Todd Turcotte, Vice President of Capital Properties, was highly critical of the position the State has taken regarding surface parking:

Figure 6.18: Graduate urban planning students from the University at Albany, being led by the author on a study tour of Providence in 2006, walking across an undeveloped parcel of Capital Center land that was being used for surface parking. (Source: Gene Bunnell)

Everyone who has developed parcels in Capital Center has dutifully followed the rules or sought variances, as the rules demand. Now to have one of the original signatories, the State no less, go forward and just do what they want seems to suggest the long established rules are porous at best (Fain, ibid.).

When interviewed in 2013, Deming Sherman made clear his opposition to the addition of more surface parking. "My view is there should be *less* parking around the State House, not more" (providencejournal.com, 2013, accessed 6/17/2015). Nevertheless, the State pushed ahead to expand surface parking on the east side of the State House. According to Ron Renaud, executive director of the Department of Administration, two tiers of parking constructed along Smith Street would take 2,000 square feet of additional grass from the lawn and create an additional 43 parking spaces. Meanwhile, the State purchased additional land along Francis Street for the purpose of building a new parking lot on the west side of the State House. If the CCC had greater financial resources at its disposal it might have considered going to court to challenge the State's action, but its limited funding has made that impossible.

Chapter Seven:

Downtown Turns the Corner

Andres Duany's 1991 Charrette

In November 1991, Andres Duany, a nationally acclaimed architect and proponent of New Urbanism, was brought to Providence, along with a team of planners and designers from Duany Plater-Zyberk & Co., to conduct a week-long master planning exercise focused on Downcity Providence. One-third of the $60,000 cost of bringing Duany and his team of planners and designers to Providence was paid by the city; two-thirds was paid by private sector donors (Smolski 1991). According to a number of people I interviewed, one of the principal private sector donors was Arnold "Buff" Chace.

Duany's typical approach when he comes into a community as an outside consultant is to hold a "charrette"—an intensive, week-long interactive process in which designers engage and interact with stakeholders, community leaders, and citizens to arrive at an agreed-upon vision for future land use and development. Duany favors this approach because it enables his design team to gain immediate feedback, and thereby progressively refine their recommendations. Throughout the week, informal meetings are held with various sub-groups related to specific issues, and updates and interim reports are issued periodically, providing participants with additional opportunities to provide feedback.

Among those who attended the 1991 charrette was Jack Yena, the President of Johnson & Wales University (JWU) in Providence. At the time, JWU had a student enrollment of 2400 students and had just converted from a junior college to a full-fledged university.[29] "The school was in the process of emerging and growing, while the city was in decline and going in the opposite direction" (Yena 2015 int.).

Yena had never heard of Andres Duany before, and wouldn't have attended had it not been for Buff Chace.

> Buff came to see me. He told me about Andres Duany, and said he was a brilliant urban planner and designer—and a very entertain-

ing speaker with a 'great delivery.' He told me Duany was going to speak twice during the charrette (on the first day, and then again on the last day) and urged me to attend (*ibid.*).

The first day of the Downcity charrette was held in an abandoned downtown building.[30] Yena recalls Duany began by saying he got the impression that people were not feeling very good about Providence, and "talked Providence down." "He said we needed to adjust our attitude and by the time he came back to speak again on the last day we would be feeling much better about our city" (*ibid.*).

Duany then provided his listeners with a short course on New Urbanism and the design qualities he and other New Urbanists believe are essential to creating and sustaining a vital city:

- Walkability: interconnected street grid;

- Hierarchy of streets: lower capacity streets ("B" streets) and higher capacity streets ("A" streets);

- Mixed-use buildings and diversity of uses;

- Mixture of housing types

- Quality architecture and urban design;

- Traditional neighborhood structure, with public space at the center;

- High quality public realm and public open space;

- Buildings, residences, shops and services close together for ease of walking;

- Pedestrian-friendly streetscapes that encourage walking and use of bicycles;

- Less reliance on automobiles, more use of public transportation and trains.

Duany said that Providence already possessed a number of the aforementioned qualities. Providence had "great buildings," and its downtown was compact and potentially one of the most walkable cities in the country. Colleges and universities in Providence were another strength of the city, although he went on to say that educational institutions, such as Brown University up on College Hill, had remained largely disengaged from the city. The one notable exception, he said, was Johnson & Wales University's presence in the downtown.

Yena says he learned a great deal from Duany's presentation. "I learned about the design qualities that help produce a pedestrian-friendly streetscape that encourages walking. I learned about the value of having a hierarchy of streets, about the difference between 'A' streets (higher capacity streets) and 'B' streets (lower capacity, service streets), and why parking garages shouldn't be located on an 'A' street. What Duany said was compelling and I came away really excited" (*ibid.*).

Yena was so inspired by Duany's presentation that he decided to retain Duany to conduct a separate charrette for Johnson & Wales University (in parallel with the Downcity charrette), for the purpose of advising the university on how and where it should expand its campus.

Duany was assisted in conducting the Downcity charrette by a team of planners and designers that included a talented architect named Randall Imai. "When people re-convened on the second day, they found that Imai had produced a series of sketches that showed what various parts of Downcity would look like if Duany's design principles were followed" (Kezirian int.).

On the last night of the four-day charrette, Duany delivered his team's findings and recommendations, in a three-hour long presentation that took place at Trinity Theater, attended by "approximately 350 enthusiastic and appreciative audience members...." (Smolski 1991).

In retrospect, by far the most important outcome produced by the Duany charrettes was JWU's decision to develop and expand its campus *in the center of downtown Providence*. As Jack Yena put it when I interviewed him, "What Johnson & Wales has done in downtown Providence has been truly catalytic. Johnson & Wales University was the catalyst."

At the time of the 1991 charrettes, JWU was considering purchasing the Regency Plaza apartment complex, which could have housed 3000 student—which in turn would have moved the center of the campus to the outer western fringe of downtown, next to Interstate 95. "The idea was to acquire the three high-rise apartment buildings, create 'green space' between them and (hopefully) eventually acquire the low-rise Cathedral apartments" (Yena, 2016 personal communication).

Duany's advice radically changed Yena's thinking, and proved providential for downtown Providence.

> Duany told us we should go in the opposite direction. 'Choose the absolute worst site in downtown and make it the best. Take the large, burnt-out Outlet Co. property, the nastiest parcel in the city, and put a signature building on it,' he said. He gave me a vision of what we could accomplish (Yena int.).

For decades, the Outlet Company occupied a full block on Weybosset Street, and dominated retail trade in Providence.[31] However, in 1982 the department store closed, and in October 1986 it was destroyed by fire. To make matters worse, the fire left behind a badly contaminated site. The fact that the site required a costly environmental cleanup presented a major obstacle to achieving the vision that Duany had conjured up for JWU.

Yena recalls going to meet with the bank that owned the Outlet Co. property in 1995. Joseph R. Paolino, Jr., Gov. Bruce Sundlun's choice as head of the state's Economic Development Corporation, also attended the meeting. Paolino's presence at the meeting proved instrumental: his involvement secured an agreement with the bank that enabled JWU to move ahead with the purchase of the property. The terms of the agreement were that the State of Rhode Island would agree to pay for the environmental cleanup of the site if Johnson & Wales agreed to buy the property and locate its campus there (Yena int.).

JWU purchased the Outlet Co. property and proceeded to develop the block and fill it in with an imposing set of buildings, making it the cornerstone of its downtown campus. The classical pillars and gates that mark the entrance to the campus were suggested by Andres Duany.

JWU purchased an adjacent building that had previously served as Broadcast House for the broadcasting empire over which Bruce Sundlun had pre-

Figure 7.1: Snowden Hall and Gaebe Commons, Johnson & Wales University downtown campus. (Source: Steve Soper, Johnson & Wales University)

Figure 7.2: Triangolo Gate, Johnson & Wales University downtown campus: a design touch suggested by Andres Duany. (Source: Patrick O'Connor, Johnson & Wales University)

Figure 7.3: View of McNulty Hall upon entering through Triangolo Gate. (Source: Gene Bunnell)

Figure 7.4: Looking across Gaebe Commons toward Yena Hall, which once housed Broadcast House of Bruce Sundlun's communications empire before he became Governor of Rhode Island. (Source: Gene Bunnell)

sided before becoming Governor. The first two floors of the building were renovated and converted into a modern library for the university.[32] Snowden Hall, on the opposite side of Gaebe Commons, was built on the site of the former St. Francis Chapel, which JWU purchased after a fire within the building.

JWU has coupled the development of its downtown campus with a community service-learning requirement, whereby students are required to devote a certain number of hours to an approved community service project. Community service is an option that is attached to various courses students might take, thereby giving students a wide range of choices in terms of subject areas. Faculty members who teach subjects that students choose to meet the service requirement are responsible for reviewing and approving the projects or experiences the students propose. They also evaluate and judge whether students have satisfactorily met the requirement.

"Johnson and Wales University has turned out to be an excellent anchor for the downtown" (Sanderson int.). By 2015, 10,000 full-time students were enrolled in nine different academic programs at JWU in Providence, in fields ranging from Business, Hospitality, and Culinary Arts to Liberal Arts, Engineering and Design, Science, and Physician Assistant Studies.

Making Downtown Redevelopment Financially Feasible

Getting private developers to invest in downtown Providence has been, and continues to be, difficult for two reasons. The first reason is that costs of construction in downtown Providence are roughly the same as those in downtown Boston, but the rents commanded by commercial and residential properties in Providence are significantly lower than those in Boston.

The second factor that discourages investment in downtown development projects is the high property tax rate in Providence, which in 2015 stood at $36.75/$1000 valuation.[33] In an attempt to reduce the extent to which high property taxes discouraged people from investing in downtown, the City of Providence enacted legislation authorizing the City to enter into "tax stabilization agreements" with prospective developers. Such tax agreements are typically entered into for 12 years. Under a typical agreement, a developer would pay no property taxes for the first 3 years. After that, property taxes would increase 10% each year for 10 years. At the end of the 12th year, the property would finally be assessed at 100% of full value.

While reducing the property taxes payable in the early years of a development project is helpful in the near term, it simply puts off the day of reckoning. "The problem is that at the end of the 12th year you're paying taxes based on full-value assessment at a tax rate of $36.75—at which point most private developments are simply not economically feasible" (Brodie int.).

State and Federal Historic Preservation Tax Credits

In 2001, Rhode Island enacted a State Historic Tax Credit Program to work in conjunction with federal historic preservation tax credits, and provide a financial incentive for renovating and restoring historic buildings. The program, which went into effect in 2002, offers state historic preservation tax credits to projects that involve the substantial renovation of income-producing properties that qualify for federal historic preservation tax credits and meet the Secretary of the Interior's *Standards for Rehabilitation*. Because Downtown Providence was placed on the National Register of Historic Places in 1984, most downtown buildings were already eligible for federal historic tax credits. As a result, once Rhode Island's state historic preservation tax credit program went into effect, buildings in the Downtown Historic District effectively became eligible for *both* federal and state tax credits.

In Providence alone, 191 substantial renovation projects, representing a total private investment of over $ 1.1 billion, qualified for state and federal tax credits between 2002 and 2015—172 of which had been completed by 2015 and 19 of which were underway but not yet completed. The substantial amount of private investment brought about by historic preservation tax credits has not been the only positive outcome. Tax credits projects have also increased the supply, and improved the quality, of housing. A total of 2381 new, high quality housing units has been created as a result of the 191 tax credit projects undertaken in Providence between 2002 and 2015.

As Ken Orenstein observed, "Tax credits have been critically important to making renovation projects feasible. Up to 50% of the cost of a project can be covered by the combination of federal and state historic preservation tax credits. No project is feasible without these tax credits" (2015 int.).

The Downtown Revolving Loan Fund

In 2000, the Rhode Island Foundation established a Downtown Revolving Fund and endowed it with $10,000,000 in funding. The Rhode Island Foundation's initial intention was to administer the loan program itself. However, deciding which projects to fund, and managing the details associated with individual projects, proved more difficult than the Foundation anticipated. Three years after establishing its Downtown Revolving Fund, the Rhode Island Foundation dissolved the fund and transferred the $7.8 million that remained to the PPS-affiliated Providence Revolving Fund.

From the beginning, the funding for downtown renovations was kept separate from the previously established Neighborhood Revolving Fund, but the two funds operate in conjunction with each other. The same staff under the direction of Clark Schoettle administers both programs. A partnership arrangement was worked out with the Providence Foundation, whereby it was agreed that the Foundation would be paid $100,000 annually to help promote and coordinate the revolving loan program with downtown property owners.

The first person willing to take on the risk of investing in a serious way in renovating downtown buildings was Arnold "Buff" Chace, the President and CEO of Cornish Associations (the person who was responsible for bringing Andres Duany to Providence in 1991). In the process of considering how to approach an earlier project in Mashpee, Massachusetts, Chace learned of Andres Duany's and DPZ's Seaside, Florida, project, and found himself drawn to the principles of New Urbanism. The project in Mashpee that Cornish Associates was about to undertake involved the redevelopment of a former strip shopping center— originally called the New Seabury Shopping Center—which included a bank, a hardware store, a florist's shop, a two-screen movie theater, a small market, a post office, and restaurant. The master plan that Cornish Associates developed for the Mashpee project called for adding internal streets, more buildings, and a wider variety of uses, including 40 residential apartments. The project, which was renamed Mashpee Commons, was widely regarded at the time as a "model of new urbanist principles in action" (O'Keefe 2006).

After completing Mashpee Commons, Chace turned his attention to downtown Providence. What he saw was a remarkably compact and walkable downtown, with an intact urban fabric and streetscape that had many of the key features of New Urbanism already built in. It occurred to Chace that rather than undertaking additional New Urbanism-inspired projects in outlying locations, a pedestrian-oriented, mixed-use New Urbanist community could be created in downtown Providence by acquiring, renovating, and converting long-neglected, largely vacant multi-story buildings.

The first project Chace undertook in downtown Providence involved the renovation and conversion of the *circa* 1912 Smith Building at 1 Fulton Street into 37 moderately-priced apartments and two commercial spaces on the ground floor—a project that was completed in 1999. In 2002, Cornish Associates completed a second project: the renovation and conversion of the seven-

Figure 7.5: The Alice Building. (Source: Cornish Associates)

story Alice Building at 236 Westminster Street (*circa* 1898) into 38 loft-style units and 5000 sq. ft. of ground-floor commercial space. The architect for both of these and for a number of subsequent renovation and conversion projects was Steve Durkee, then a principal of the architectural firm of Durkee Brown Viveiros and Werenfels. Durkee later joined Cornish Associates.

Between 2004 and 2005, Cornish Associates renovated five additional buildings in close proximity to the Smith and Alice Buildings. Two previously distinct structures, the 1925 O'Gorman Building at 220 Westminster Street and the 1890 Burgess Building around the corner at 89 Eddy Street were combined and renovated to produce a total of 30 new downtown housing units (17 apartments in the O'Gorman Building and 13 loft-style units in the Burgess Building, including two penthouse units on the top two floors). Renovation of the Wilkinson Building (*circa* 1900) at 90 Eddy Street produced another 12 upper-story apartments with retail on the ground floor. The fifth and largest of this cluster of building conversions involved the former Peerless Department Store building at 150 Union Street, which was renovated at a cost of $42 million to accommodate 97 loft apartments, a 68-car parking garage in the basement, ground-floor retail, and a rooftop terrace with a green roof.

Figure 7.6: The Burgess-O'Gorman Building is on the near corner of this Westminster Street block; the Alice Building is at the far end of the block. (Source: Cornish Associates)

Figure 7.7: Wilkinson Building before renovation. (Source: Providence Revolving Fund)

Figure 7.8: Wilkinson Building after renovation. (Source: Providence Revolving Fund

Figure 7.9: Exterior view of Peerless Building. (Source: Cornish Associates)

Figure 7.10: Peerless Building apartment interior. (Source: Cornish Associates)

Figure 7.11: Peerless Building apartment interior. (Source: Cornish Associates)

In November 2015 Cornish Associates completed the renovation of the Kinsley Building in the 400 block of Westminster Street. By April 2016, all 44 of the apartments in the building, one-bedroom and studio apartments ranging in size from 400 to 550 sq. ft., were under contract. By the middle of 2016, Cornish Associates had single-handedly produced a total of 240 new downtown housing units.

Additional downtown renovation/conversion projects have been undertaken by other developers, such as the renovation of the Palmer Building at 100 Fountain Street into 12 housing units with ground-floor retail; and the renovation of the building at 79 Washington Street that formerly housed the historic Strand Theater. The "Lofts at the Strand" produced 20 new downtown condominiums. One of the largest and most dramatic building reuse projects, known as "Providence G", involved the renovation of four adjacent but previously separate buildings: the Providence Gas Building; an addition built by National Grid; the garage of the former Narragansett Hotel; and the Teste Building. Located at 100 Dorrance Street, the project produced 56 one- and two-bedroom apartment units, a popular lower-level pub and casual dining establishment, a ground-level coffee shop, a more formal all-season rooftop restaurant, a ballroom, and an attached 60-car parking garage.

One of the most unusual downtown building conversions involved the historic 1828 Arcade building at 65 Weybosset Street, a project that was com-

Figure 7.12: This block of buildings on Dorrance Street was renovated as part of the Providence G project. (Source: Gene Bunnell)

Figure 7.13: Renovated apartment interior in the Teste Building, part of the Providence G project. (Source: Providence Revolving Fund)

Figure 7.14: Arcade Building entrance fronting on Westminster Street. (Source: Gene Bunnell)

Figure 7.15: Side view of renovated Arcade Building that shows windows of upper floor micro-housing units. (Source: Gene Bunnell)

pleted in 2014. More than once during the past four decades, the Arcade stood vacant; and more than once, it was threatened with demolition. The building became vacant most recently in 2008, after which it remained vacant for four years. The Providence Preservation Society placed the building on its list of the Top Ten Endangered Properties in 2009.

The classic ground-floor shopping arcade of the Arcade Building extends all the way through the building from Westminster Street to Weybosset Street, with Greek Revival-style columns framing formal entrances from both streets. Back in the nineteenth and early twentieth century, such arcades were extremely popular places to shop. But by the latter half of the twentieth century, with the development of outlying shopping plazas and the general decline of downtown, the small shops that lined the arcade struggled to attract customers.

The developer who successfully renovated the Arcade Building, Evan Granoff, recognized that ground-floor retail could no longer generate sufficient rents to justify and financially support the cost of renovating the building. He therefore did something truly unconventional. He developed the upper two floors of the building into 50 micro-loft units 250-300 sq. ft. in floor area. These small residential units rented immediately, and there remains a long waiting list.

In 2015, the occupancy rate of downtown housing units was running at around 95%. "We're up to 4,000 people living downtown. Occupancy rates of downtown housing units are very high. I wish we had more downtown housing units available for occupancy," said Dan Badouin, Executive Director of the Providence Foundation.

Nurturing Ground Floor Commercial Activity

When Cornish Associates first began converting former commercial buildings to housing they faced a challenge in marketing the newly created housing units analogous to the classic question, "Which came first: the chicken or the egg?" Who wants to live in a downtown where there are few, if any, stores selling goods and services needed on a regular basis, nowhere to buy groceries and fresh produce, and few good (and reasonably-priced) places to eat and drink? Conversely, who wants to open and operate a commercial establishment in an area with a small customer base?

By the time the first residents moved into upper-story downtown housing units, almost all of the retail and service establishments that had formerly operated in the downtown had closed years before. Indeed, the limited number and poor quality of the businesses that remained posed a major impediment to enticing more people to live downtown.

Buff Chace recognized the importance of filling the vacant ground floors of downtown buildings, and creating a more stimulating and engaging pedestrian environment. "The more businesses there are downtown, the more pedestrian activity there will be, and the more appealing downtown will be as a place to live" (Chace int.). He also felt it was important to try to fill ground floor spaces with one-of-a-kind, locally-owned businesses that would lend a unique quality to downtown and add to its appeal. The problem was that the entrepreneurs willing to consider opening and operating a business in one of Cornish's buildings were often starting up a new business, had little prior business experience or track record, and were under-capitalized. Such start-up businesses had difficulty obtaining bank financing and couldn't afford to commit to paying a standard market rent.

To enable such small, locally owned businesses to commit to occupying street-level downtown commercial space, Cornish structured the rent per month as a percentage of receipts, rather than as a fixed amount. Such an arrangement enabled the "Queen of Hearts" dress shop to occupy ground floor retail space in the O'Gorman Building. Similar lease agreements have been entered into with other businesses on Westminster Street.

Chace, and Cornish Associates, also played an important role in getting a grocery/convenience store to locate and operate in downtown. Cornish signed a master lease with Rhode Island School of Design for the ground floor of the multi-story building it owned at the corner of Weybosset and Union Streets, the upper floors of which housed the school's painting and photography studios. The location of the building was ideal, inasmuch as it was directly across the street from Johnson & Wales University's downtown campus.

Once it secured the master lease, Cornish went looking for a company with experience in operating a grocery that served a university community, and found one that was operating in New Haven. The operator of that business agreed to lease the space and open a second business in Providence, called Serendipity Gourmet. In addition to selling fresh produce, baked goods and groceries, Serendipity Gourmet also offers a hot food take-out buffet. "After a number of years of successful operation, the distributor that provided organic foods to the store has taken over the space, and is looking forward to expanding (Chace int.)."

On a vacant lot at the corner of Westminster and Union Streets, Cornish Associates installed a bocce court. It also hung a large white screen on the side of the building overlooking the lot for showing movies. On a sunny day in April 2016, a group of young children under the watchful eyes of parents or day-care providers were making use of the bocce court's lot as a playground.

Meanwhile, Cornish Associates bought the building at 276 Westminster

Street which had formerly housed the Black Repertory Theater and later Roots Café, and reopened it as a flexible performing and event space. "We didn't want it to become a bad nightclub and have a negative influence on the area in which we have so heavily invested (Chace int.)." Chace named the venue "Aurora," after the Roman goddess of the new dawn. Aurora opened in May 2014. In April 2015, Chrissy Wolpert was hired by Chace to manage the space, which has a license to sell beer, wine and liquor, but not a license to serve food.

During her first year in charge of managing Aurora, Wolpert has explored the potential of the space by introducing different types of programs and uses. Monthly "Variety Shows" have been held at Aurora, and the first Wednesday of every month is Salsa Night. "The salsa music is incredible, and people really enjoy themselves," says Wolpert. Aurora also now has its own resident theater company, the Burbage Theater Company, which as of May 2016 had performed two productions in the space. As I was interviewing Wolpert by telephone, a high school group could be heard in the background, doing sound checks for a production they were going to present in the space that night.

"We've hosted a lot of different types of music, had poetry readings, and rented out the space for community social events and discussion groups," said Wolpert. "We're still experimenting. People can come to us with an idea, and we'll give it a try and see if there is an audience."

Figure 7.16: Aurora, 276 Westminster Street (Source: Gene Bunnell)

To date, Aurora has functioned primarily as a nightspot, typically opening at 5:00 PM, and staying open until 1:00 AM Sunday through Thursday, and until 2:00 AM on Friday and Saturday. In the future, however, Aurora may be open more often during the day. When the New England Chapter of the Congress for the New Urbanism held an "Urbanism Summit" in Providence in April, 2016, Aurora was where the attendees first gathered.

Cornish Associates has been remarkably patient in terms of earning a return on its investments. Rather than expecting to make a quick profit, the company has been investing in downtown Providence for the long term. "Outside development companies and investors would not have had the patience to stick this approach over such a long period" (Chace int.). It has taken a long time for this approach to bear fruit, but by 2016 it appears that Downcity has turned the corner, with 49 ground-floor businesses in operation, including an upscale, well-stocked wine and liquor store to meet the needs of the growing number of downtown residents.

Impacts of the Downtown Revolving Fund

By 2015, the Downtown Revolving Fund had made loans and grants totaling roughly $13 million toward the cost of renovating/converting 23 downtown buildings, leveraging $132 million in private investment in the process. For example, a number of the previously mentioned downtown building conversions received loans from the PRF, such as the Wilkinson Building ($500,000 loan), the Peerless Building ($1 million loan), and the Teste Building, part of the Providence G project ($500,000 loan). As has been the case with the Neighborhood Revolving Fund, loan defaults associated with the Downtown Revolving Fund have been low—only $306,000 since 2003.

Making loans and small incentive grants is not the only way in which the Revolving Fund has supported renovation activity in downtown Providence. The staff of the Revolving Fund has provided design assistance to downtown building owners and developers, and helped pay for feasibility studies and other pre-development costs. It has also served as the Historic Tax Credit consultant on a number of projects, thereby enabling those projects to qualify for federal and state historic preservation tax credits which have been crucial to making them financially feasible. In certain cases, PRF has also provided gap financing in the form of loans against, and in anticipation of, federal and state historic tax credits which will come later.

One particularly noteworthy project for which the PRF served as Historic Tax Credit consultant involved the renovation and reuse of the former Browne and Sharpe foundry buildings on the north side of the downtown, which had stood vacant for roughly 20 years. PRF didn't need to put any money into the project, but the staff of the PRF advised the architects and owner of the complex on how the project could meet the National Parks Service's standards, and thereby qualify for federal historic preservation tax credits (which qualification, as explained previously, is the pre-condition for also qualifying for state historic preservation tax credits). The completed project, known as the Promenade, contains a total of 433 studio, one-bedroom and two-bedroom apartments: 237 units in one building and 196 units in the other.

Figure 7.17: Interior of apartment at the Promenade, with the Rhode Island State House visible through the window. (Source: Providence Revolving Fund)

In a few instances the Downtown Revolving Fund has played a more direct role in rescuing buildings. "We have sometimes done 'turn-key' projects in partnership with developers who have agreed to forego their developers' fee and commit it toward the cost of the project. We did this with regard to the renovation/conversion of the Arnold Building downtown" (Schoettle int.).

The time and effort the Revolving Fund expended trying to save the Arnold Building demonstrates the lengths to which preservationists in Providence have sometimes been willing to go to safeguard the city's architectural

Figure 7.18: Arnold Building before being renovated. (Source: Erik Lubrick, AS220)

Figure 7.19: Narrow side of the Arnold Building viewed from Matthewson Street.
(Source: Gene Bunnell)

heritage. The Arnold Building was built in 1923 on the corner of Washington and Mathewson Streets, and is distinguished by the fact that it is 120 feet long on the Washington Street side, but only 12 ½ feet deep on the side facing Mathewson Street—making it by far the narrowest and shallowest building in the city. By the 1990s the building had become increasingly run-down.

> After the building behind it was demolished for a parking lot, the Arnold Building's future became less secure, as did its structural integrity. By 2005, The Providence Revolving Fund had become concerned about the condition of the rear wall, and initiated conversations with [the owner regarding] improvements to stabilize the building. After a year of negotiation, [the owner] agreed to make improvements if the Revolving Fund would participate with a small matching grant and favorable loan... Work was progressing, the back wall was being repaired, a fire alarm system was installed—I was feeling optimistic.

> Then, on an afternoon in 2009 a fire broke out on the 3rd floor which nearly destroyed the east side of the building. It became clear we had a real problem. At this point, [the owner] wanted to get his insurance proceeds, lost interest in the project, and sold the property (Schoettle int.).

After a year of the building being under new ownership, it became clear to the Schoettle and PRF that the building could not be saved under its then current owner.

> Luckily, Don Gralnick had joined the City as Director of the PRA and was game to help. We suggested that the PRA should condemn the property and take it by eminent domain (something that had not been done since the 1990s). If the PRA would do that, the Revolving Fund would agree to purchase the building and renovate it for reuse ... During the 2-year process of finalizing the condemnation, Dave Stern... came through my door and expressed his interest in developing it. I suggested we consider a partnership [involving] PRF, Dave, and his wife Lori Quinn. We worked up the numbers and put together a *pro forma* for the $800,000 project. We filled in the gaps with various loans from the PRF Downcity Fund. We also obtained additional support from state and federal historic tax credits, and the Planning Department helped out in the form of

Figure 7.20: Renovated upper floor apartment in the Arnold Building
(Source: Providence Revolving Fund)

grants from HUD to create two affordable housing units upstairs.

We purchased the building in December 2013, and here we are two and a half years later ... We really performed a miracle and prevented a huge loss to the streetscape of Providence (Schoettle, 2016 personal communication).

An Organization of Artists Enriches Downtown

An investment in the arts and culture is a way to improve a community's livability while boosting its economy.
— Times Union (Albany, NY) editorial, July 16, 2016

Providence's downtown today is home to a remarkable artists-run organization, called AS220, which as of 2016 owned three separate downtown buildings containing a total of 100,000 square feet of floor space, and was in the process of working to acquire two more downtown buildings. The buildings

AS220 owns and manages typically contain artist studios, live/work studios, and apartments on the top floors; restaurants, bars, cafes and other commercial uses on the ground floor; and 9-to-5 business on the second floor to buffer the two. Within the three buildings AS220 now owns and manages, there are currently four dozen artist live/work studios, and a dozen individual work studios. There are also four exhibition spaces; a performance space; a "black-box" theater; a dance studio; a print shop; a community darkroom; a digital media lab; a high-tech fabrication lab; a recording studio; and a space devoted to a youth program.

The person widely acknowledged to have been the force behind the creation of AS220, and largely responsible for its creation and evolution is Umberto "Bert" Crenca. The event that caused Crenca to want to establish an artist-run organization like AS220 took place in 1983. "Back in 1983," Crenca explains, "Providence was regarded as 'the armpit of New England.' Back in 1983, Providence didn't look like it does now. Everyone wanted to get out of Providence" (Crenca, TEDx Providence 2013).

Crenca was 33 years old, a young, aspiring artist at the time, and was given the opportunity to exhibit his paintings publicly for the first time at a local gallery. By his own account, he thought he was a pretty good artist, and looked forward to having his paintings positively received.

The paintings he exhibited were not only stylistically bold; they plumbed the depths of social and political commentary, and expressed Crenca's outrage at social and political injustices he found deeply disturbing. Channing Gray, the art critic for *The Providence Journal*, wrote a scathing review of Crenca's paintings. Gray began his review by saying, "Using art as a vehicle for social commentary is a risky proposition at best" (Cook, 2014). Crenca can't forget the stinging phrases the art critic used to belittle his paintings: "No injustice escapes his notice ... with a few globs of flesh-colored paint and a handful of old chicken bones" (TEDx Providence 2013).

"I was absolutely crushed," says Crenca. In the wake of this blow to his self-confidence as an artist, he brought together a group of around 15 local artists who began meeting regularly at Crenca's home, talking and arguing about what was needed to create a vibrant arts community in Providence. Among the people in the group were Steve Emma, Martha Dempster, Scott Seabolt, and Susan Clausen. After months of debate and back-and-forth discussion, they finalized and issued a position paper they called a "Manifesto," which they sent to every media outlet Rhode Island, except *The Providence Journal*. The central message of the Manifesto was that for art to flourish artists needed more opportunities to show their works without being approved of by self-appointed art critics and juries of so-called art experts.

Below is a short excerpt of the strongly-worded 1983 Manifesto:

> We challenge the assumption that an art degree, education, position, or monetary success, necessarily legitimizes an artist's endeavors, opinions, judgments, or give credence to an artist's work!

> We challenge the award system with their self-congratulatory aggrandizement that fosters the false premise that the winning of awards, prizes, grants, and so on necessarily validates an artist's work, position, judgement or opinion.

> We challenge the pervasive notion that complete unbridled, uncensored freedom produces mediocrity and that excellence rises out of repression. It does not!

Figure 7.21: Umberto "Bert" Crenca, principal founder of AS220.[34]

Crenca decided he needed to travel to and spend time in Italy and other European cities studying the classic, highly revered art works produced in earlier eras. Upon returning to Providence, Crenca reconnected with his fellow artist friends and used his last $800 to lease space on the second floor of the Providence Performing Arts Center. The group decided to call itself AS220. AS stood for "Alternative Space"; the number 220 was derived from the street address of the Performing Arts Center, which was 220 Weybosset Street. "We did a lot of crazy things in the space, and made a lot of noise. After a few months we got a letter that essentially said 'We think what you are doing is important, but you need to do it somewhere else" (Crenca, TEDx Providence 2013).

The group went on from there to rent space in a building on Richmond Street behind the Performing Arts Center.

After a few years of being on Richmond Street, we started talking about owning our own building. In 1992 we bought 95-121
Empire Street. It was in horrific condition, having been occupied
by porn shops and other illicit activities. There was no electricity,
no heat. The roof leaked, and the floors were warped and buck-
led. We paid $100,000 for the building, and had to spend another
$400,000 renovating the building to make it usable. It was a pretty
audacious move for an organization that had so few assets at the
time. Three Providence banks agreed to enter into a partnership
arrangement to jointly share the risk of financing the renovation.
The risk was considerable because we were a rag-tag group of artists who couldn't offer any collateral (Crenca int.).

AS220's initial renovation of its Empire Street building was of necessity
limited to addressing its most glaring problems and deficiencies. Between 2004
and 2006, a fund-raising campaign launched by AS220 raised $2 million, which
enabled it to significantly upgrade the Empire Street building.

In 2006, AS220 purchased the former Dreyfus Hotel on the corner of
Washington and Mathewson Street from Johnson & Wales University. Within
a year it had completed renovating the building, with a grant of $10,000 and
a storefront loan of $19,000 from the Providence Revolving Fund. The build-
ing now contains 10 studios, 14 apartments, the AS220 Project Space Gallery,
AS220's administrative offices, and *Local 121*, a farm-to-table restaurant.

In 2008, AS220 purchased its third and largest downtown building, the
four-story, 50,000 sq. ft. Mercantile Block at 131 Washington Street, and renovated it so that it now contains 10 live/work studios, 22 apartments, work-
shops and printmaking studios, and 5 ground-floor retail/commercial spaces.
The Providence Revolving Fund helped finance the renovation by providing a
$500,000 loan and a $40,000 grant toward the cost of the $11,600,000 project.

Channing Gray, who, over 30 years ago, wrote the scathing review of Bert
Crenca's paintings, still writes for *The Providence Journal*. With the passage of
time, Crenca appears to have largely forgiven Gray for his cruel review. Gray is
inclined to look on the bright side. "Who knew a few caustic words about a
painting show would lead to the creation of a beloved arts institution" (Gray, as
quoted by Cook, 2014).

Figure 7.22: AS 220s presence has revitalized and brought a once seedy block of Empire Street back to life.
(Source: Gene Bunnell)

Figure 7.23: Bar and bistro, called FOO(D), on ground floor of AS220's Empire Street building.
(Source: Erik Lubrick, AS220)

Figure 7.24: AS220 Dreyfus Hotel. (Source: Providence Revolving Fund)

Figure 7.25: AS 220's Mercantile Block (Source: Gene Bunnell)

Figure 7.26: September 2015 AS220 Gallery Opening.
(Source: Edwin Pastor, AS220)

Figure 7.27: AS220 Printmaking Studio-- large block print produced by John McKaig.
(Source: AS220)

Figure 7.28: AS220 Silk Screen Studio. (Source: AS220)

Figure 7.29: Drink + Ink 2016-- printing a slogan that pretty much sums up the attitude of AS220.
(Source: AS220)

Figure 7.30: Art increasingly in evidence: mural on side of building overlooking parking lot along 400 block of Westminster Street. (Source: Gene Bunnell)

Chapter Eight:

Relocating Interstate 195 and
Stitching the Downtown Area Back Together

The 1992 Old Harbor Plan

The highway engineers who chose the original alignment for I-195 could not have done a better job in dividing downtown Providence. As built in the 1950s, I-195 slashed through historic neighborhoods, separated the Fox Point neighborhood from its waterfront, and cut the Jewelry District off from the rest of downtown.

By the 1990s, I-195 had reached the end of its useful life, and needed to be entirely reconstructed, including a new bridge across the Providence River. Highway engineers at RIDOT in charge of developing plans for reconstructing I-195 had assumed that the highway alignment would remain the same as in the past, and that the new bridge over the Providence River would be built either slightly north or slightly south of the old bridge.

William Warner's Waterfront Study produced a finding that eventually brought about a fundamental re-thinking of the project. Warner found that if access ramps leading to and from I-195 at Old Harbor were relocated, approximately 44 acres along both sides of the Providence River would be freed up for more productive use, including open space and water-related uses beneficial to adjacent neighborhoods. The engineering and design contract for rebuilding I-195 had already been entered into with the firm of C. E. Maguire. Nevertheless, Joseph Arruda, who headed RIDOT's Planning Division, recommended that RIDOT hold off putting the I-195 project out to bid while further studies were conducted.

In 1991, Robert E. Freeman, who had succeeded Ken Orenstein as executive director of the Providence Foundation, went through very much the same process that Warner and Orenstein had gone through years earlier to launch the Providence Waterfront Study. This time, the aim was to prepare a plan covering the entire Old Harbor area, including the possibility of relocating

I-195 rather than merely relocating the access ramps at Old Harbor. The plan would also recommend land use policies for the area freed up by the highway relocation. Freeman and Warner worked together to prepare and submit this new NEA grant application, which once again was successful. Johnson & Wales University also contributed $10,000 toward the cost of the study (Yena int.).

The *Old Harbor Plan* was completed in 1992. The plan identified two alternatives: rebuild I-195 along its original alignment, or shift I-195 to the south, to a location just south of the Hurricane Barrier.[35] Once again, Pete Pointner was brought in to assist the Maguire group and Warner in preparing the EIS that evaluated the two highway alternatives. In 1996, the final EIS was completed and concluded that the Hurricane Barrier alignment was the best solution. Relocating I-195 south of the Hurricane Barrier would not only improve traffic flow and safety, but would also repair the damage done to inner-city neighborhoods by the original alignment. The newly chosen highway alignment also meant that construction of the new highway could proceed while the existing highway remained in use, thereby reducing traffic disruptions.

Few cities have the opportunity to redevelop vacant land in their core areas without demolishing existing buildings and displacing long-time residents or businesses. Having already been presented with one such opportunity by relocating the Northeast Rail Corridor, Providence was about to be presented with another opportunity to redevelop a fairly large amount of vacant land on the edge of its downtown due to the impending relocation of I-195.

City officials, planners, and various stakeholders had plenty of time to think about how the vacant land freed up by dismantling the former I-195 right-of-way should be redeveloped. The decision to relocate I-195 was effectively arrived at in 1992, when William Warner's Old Harbor plan was completed and adopted; actual construction work related to relocating I-195 began only in 2002. It took another ten years, until 2012, to complete the project, and finish the job of dismantling and removing old portions of I-195.

The 1999 Jewelry District Concept Plan

In 1997, the Jewelry District Association (JDA) was established: a non-profit organization composed of property owners, businesses, and people who lived and worked in the Jewelry District. In 1999, the JDA hired Thompson Design Group of Boston to help it develop a concept plan to guide the future development of the district. A charrette was conducted that involved not only members the JDA but also other stakeholders. Among the individuals and organizations involved in the process were John Palmieri, Director of Plan-

Figure 8.1: Illustrated aerial photo showing I-195 as originally constructed, and proposed new I-195 alignment and river crossing. Also shown: the boundaries of the Jewelry District and Downcity, and the area between the Jewelry District and Downcity most directly and negatively impacted by the original alignment of I-195. (Source: Providence Department of Planning and Development)

ning; Thomas Deller, Deputy Director of Planning; Ken Orenstein, Orenstein Real Estate Services; Barbara Walzer, Southside/Broad Street Program; Harry Bilodeau, Fox Point Neighborhood Assoc.; Stanley Weiss, Downcity Merchants Assoc.; and Daniel Baudouin, Providence Foundation. Many others, too numerous to list here, also participated in the process.

At the time the Concept Plan was prepared, no new construction had taken place in the Jewelry District for over 65 years, except for two private parking garages. Surface parking dominated the district, scattered amid and surrounding various manufacturing buildings. However, the plan noted that a number of former manufacturing buildings had been modified to become residential lofts and office space. The vision of the future put forward in the plan was that the Jewelry District could:

> ... extend the Renaissance of Downtown Providence ... and provide the Providence community with an alternative urban environment within which to live and work .... In addition, the District's water frontage has the potential to ... extend and unify parklands along the water with a continuous water's edge walkway and "Providence River Parkway".... (Jewelry District Concept Plan, 8-9).

The plan set out five goals for the district, which were:

- A Design-Arts Capital: a place where designers and design-related businesses continue to locate, and where outdoor art and public art define the district;

- A Vital Medium-Density Neighborhood: with increasing numbers of residents, employees and visitors, and a development climate that makes new construction as well as renovations of existing buildings possible;

- A Place Where It's Fun to Walk: with buildings oriented to the street to promote variety and interest, and a rich mix of uses along the sidewalk that encourages exploration on foot;

- A Waterfront Gateway to the Atlantic Ocean: a district focused on the waterfront around Heritage Harbor Museum and Davol Square;

- A Distinct Identity: with an eclectic mix of uses that provides freedom for design innovation, and ... inspiration for the design of new projects.

Andres Duany Returns to Providence: The 2004 Charrette

In 2004, Andres Duany and designers and architects from DPZ were brought back to Providence to conduct a second charrette focused on Downcity. As in 1991, Arnold "Buff" Chace was instrumental in providing financial support for the event, but this time Chace was joined by a long list of other sponsors and financial contributors, which included the City of Providence, the Providence Foundation, Rhode Island Housing, Kim and Liz Chace, The

Chace Fund, Wellington Trust Company, Bank Rhode Island, Brown University, Johnson & Wales University, Rhode Island School of Design, and Roger Williams University—Downtown Campus.

"Nearly 500 people crowded into the ballroom at the top of the Biltmore Hotel on March 11 to hear Andres Duany tell how downtown Providence—already one of America's most walkable city centers—should build on its strengths" (*New Urban News*, posted online 1 April 2004). What Duany presented that night was also summarized in the 27-page report, "Connecting and Completing Downcity".

By the time this second charrette was held in 2004, construction work had begun on relocating Interstate 195. The opportunities and challenges that would be faced in stitching the downtown back together once the older portion of I-195 was removed, were therefore very much on people's minds. Duany urged that the City act proactively to "complete Downcity" by requiring that new buildings built in the Jewelry District and the former I-195 corridor have a considerable amount of street frontage, and have activity-generating uses on their ground floors to create an engaging streetscape for pedestrians.

The 2008 Jewelry District/Old Harbor Planning Framework Study

Six years after construction began on the relocation of I-195, the Jewelry District Association and Providence Foundation sponsored a second study, aimed at further refining and shaping the land use policies that would apply to a much larger geographic area than was focused on by the 1999 Jewelry District Concept Plan. The boundaries of this enlarged study area were formed by Downcity on the north, the Providence River to the east, and the Hurricane Barrier and planned new right-of-way of I-195 to the south. Specifically included in the study area was the land that would be freed up when the old portion of I-195 was removed, as well as adjacent blocks of the downtown affected by the roadway's realignment. The consultant team hired to conduct the study was composed of The Cecil Group of Boston, Economics Research Associates, and Maguire Group.

Institutions, businesses, property owners and public officials, as well as people living and working in the area, were invited to participate in the planning process. A 17-member Steering Committee was established, chaired by Richard Jaffe of the Davol Square Jewelry Mart Corporation. The Steering Committee included six residents, as well as representatives of Brown University; the Providence Foundation; Johnson & Wales University; the Rhode Island Histor-

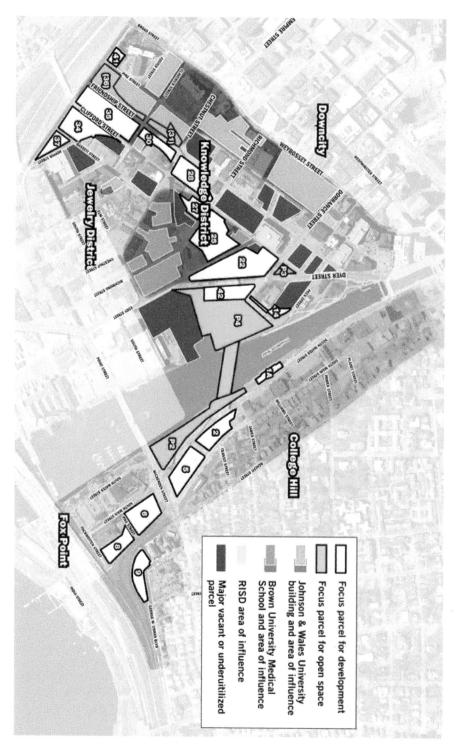

Figure 8.2: Map of parcels within the former I-195 corridor slated for development, as well as parcels on opposite sides of the Providence River reserved for parks and open space. Areas of Downcity and the former Jewelry District adjacent to the I-195 District are also shown. (Source: Providence Department of Planning and Development)

ical Preservation and Heritage Commission; and major health care institutions and employers in the area. Also included as *ex officio* members of the Steering Committee were Thomas Deller (Director of Planning and Development of the city); Steve Durkee (Chair of the City Plan Commission); City Council member Ernie Hutton; and representatives of RIDOT and RIEDC. Two public forums were also help to solicit input and comment.

Like the 1999 Concept Plan, the report produced by the 2008 study argued that the mixed-use character of the area should be viewed as a strength, and that a combination of commercial, residential, cultural, and institutional uses should be encouraged to add to the area's mixed-use character. Like the earlier plan, the 2008 study also called for creating a pedestrian-oriented district, and for strengthening pedestrian connections within the district, to the riverfront and to neighboring areas of the city. The two documents differ in that the 2008 study identified specific ways in which the desired ends could be attained.

One of the most valuable aspects of the 2008 Framework Study report was a section in which the consultant team examined and analyzed the experience of four comparable mixed-use districts in other cities. Its purpose was to investigate the approaches that other communities employed in the development of neighborhoods with similar characteristics and conditions. In each of the districts selected, the mix of uses included institutional, life sciences or bio-tech research and development. Each of districts selected was also in close proximity to a downtown or urban core that had been the subject of initiatives undertaken by both the public sector and institutions. The four districts studied were: South Lake Union in Seattle; New East Side/East Baltimore in Baltimore; University Park in Cambridge, Massachusetts; and Virginia Biotechnology Research Park in Richmond.

One of the study's most important findings was that, in each of the four mixed-use districts, there was substantial and sustained public sector involvement (city and, often, state) in achieving the desired mix of land uses and pattern of development: a finding that was all the more important because, up to that point, the public sector had exerted remarkably little leadership in promoting plans and policies to guide the future development of Providence's Jewelry District/Old Harbor area. Rather, the leadership and initiative for establishing plans to guide how the area should be developed had come almost entirely from the private sector.

Drawing on insights gained by examining experience elsewhere, the Jewelry District/Old Harbor Framework Study recommended the following specific actions:

- A district master plan and rezoning effort to permit and encourage mixed-use development;

- A plan for the I-195 parcels;

- An open space plan and implementation strategy to create a connected series of parks and open spaces;

- A collaborative effort to create a distinctively designed pedestrian bridge across the river;

- A parking plan and parking development strategy for structured parking at key locations;

- Development incentives to support the creation of a mixture of uses, including residential, neighborhood retail and cultural activities;

- Strategies for improving roadway conditions, streetscape and transit service;

- Coordinated actions to ensure management, maintenance and sustainability of public spaces and infrastructure.

The I-195 Commission

In November 2011, "An Act Relating to Public Property and Works (H5994)" was passed by the Rhode Island General Assembly. The Act called for the creation of a seven-member commission, appointed by the governor, to plan and oversee the redevelopment of the land formerly occupied by I-195.[36] The Act also directed the Rhode Island Economic Development Corporation (RIEDC) to issue up to $40 million in bonds to acquire the land formerly occupied by I-195 from the Federal Highway Administration on behalf of the I-195 Commission.

The powers granted to the I-195 Commission were greater than those granted to the Capital Center Commission. The I-195 Commission could acquire real property, subdivide or merge lots, and sell or lease property. It was also given broad powers regarding zoning administration and the permitting of development. Development taking place on former I-195 land needed to be consistent with the City of Providence Comprehensive Plan and Zoning Ordinances, but "the Commission shall serve as the sole permitting authority for all development within the district."

Figure 8.3: Vacant land within the former I-195 corridor slated for development in April 2016, outlined by granite blocks. (Source: Gene Bunnell)

The I-195 Commission legislation listed specific types of development that were deemed appropriate to take place within the I-195 corridor: institutional and residential development; education and training; knowledge-based jobs in industries such as research and development and life sciences; media technologies; entrepreneurship and business management; software design and application; and other uses consistent with a knowledge-based economy. The legislation also included a provision that requires developers of I-195 land to undertake and complete their development projects within a strict time-frame. Once the I-195 Commission approves the sale of an I-195 parcel, construction must begin no later than one year after the date of sale, and must be completed no later than three years after that date.

Removing old portions of I-195 freed up a total of 69 acres of land, but that land lacked the kinds of basic infrastructure needed to support development. In 2013, RIDOT prepared a subdivision plan that showed where new street rights-of-way were to be established. Once the land required for the new rights-of-way was subtracted from the total, approximately 22 acres of potentially developable land remained. These 22 acres were further subdivided by the I-195 Commission into 18 parcels of land slated to be marketed for development, and two parcels located on opposite sides of the Providence River which were reserved for parks and open space.

In 2014, the I-195 Commission hired Goody Clancy, a Boston-based planning and design firm, to prepare a "Tool Kit" for developers interested in developing land within the I-195 corridor. The Tool Kit was issued in February 2014 and posted online on the I-195 Commission's website.

Not long after Rhode Island Governor Gina Raimondo took office in January 2015, she appointed seven new members to the I-195 Commission. She also pushed through a 2015 state budget that included $25 million earmarked for the purpose of providing gap financing to worthy projects in the I-195 district. The newly approved state budget also authorized and made available a Rebuild Rhode Island Tax Credit to provide an additional incentive for development. In September 2015, Peter McNally replaced Jan Brodie as Executive Director of the I-195 Commission.

The 2012 Providence Downtown and Knowledge District Plan

It is difficult to say exactly when and how the term "Knowledge District" was first applied to the combined areas of the I-195 District, Jewelry District and Old Harbor area. What is clear is that this "re-branding" of the area was cemented by the Office of Planning and Development's 2012 *Providence Downtown and Knowledge District Plan*.[37]

Few new ideas were presented in this 2012 plan. Rather, its importance is that it brought together many of the ideas and proposals that had been endorsed during the 1999 and 2008 privately sponsored planning processes. Like the earlier plans, the Knowledge District plan called for increasing public access to the Providence River, for extending walkways south along both sides of the river, and for creating a "Waterfront Park" on the 8-acre parcel of former I-195 land that had been reserved for that purpose. Like the 2008 Jewelry District/Old Harbor Framework Study, it also called for a pedestrian bridge to be built to connect the park to open space on the opposite side of the river. Concrete footings that formerly supported I-195 when it crossed the Providence River at that point will be used to support the new pedestrian bridge, thereby reducing the cost of construction.

A design competition was held in 2011 to come up with an imaginative design for the pedestrian/bicycle bridge. The winning design of the Providence River Pedestrian Bridge Competition was submitted by inFORM Studio of Northville, Michigan.

Figure 8.4: Extension of Riverwalk along the west side of the Providence River up to the site of the proposed Waterfront Park. (Source: Gene Bunnell)

Figure 8.5: Winning design for Providence River pedestrian bridge. (Source: Providence Department of Planning and Development)

Revised Zoning

In 2012, Mayor Angel Taveras announced that the City of Providence had adopted revised zoning regulations for the Knowledge District, which he said would provide more predictable guidelines for the development (Nickerson, www.gcpvd.org May 16, 2012).[38]

As a result of the 2012 zoning revision, substantially the same zoning that applies to Downcity now applies to the I-195 and Jewelry Districts as well. "Interstate 195 used to separate the Jewelry District from Downcity, and the highway was the zoning district boundary that separated the D1 Zone (Downcity) from the D2 Zone in the Jewelry District. Once the interstate was gone, the zoning discrepancies between the adjacent areas no longer made sense" (Azar int.).

The zoning that formerly applied throughout the Knowledge District, which called for warehouses and industry, was essentially hostile to mixed use development. The zoning now in effect encourages mixed-use development, by providing an incentive for developers to incorporate restaurants, retail, cultural or entertainment facilities, and other uses on the ground floors of buildings. Projects which include such activity-generating ground floor uses can qualify for a density bonus of up to 30% over and above what would otherwise be allowed. Urban design provisions that formerly applied only to the downtown now also apply more broadly throughout the Knowledge District, the aim being to create a more pedestrian-friendly urban fabric and streetscape.

According to Robert Azar, Deputy Director of Providence's Department of Planning and Development, many of the requirements and standards incorporated into the revised zoning were recommended by Andres Duany during his 2004 and 1991 charrettes. One of the most important of these new provisions is that demolition of existing buildings is allowed only upon applying for and obtaining a waiver from the city's Design Review Committee—a waiver subject to strict criteria. In effect, an applicant wanting to demolish an existing structure must present plans showing what will be built in its place.

Among the design standards and requirements now incorporated into the zoning ordinance are:

- "Build-to" frontage requirements to strengthen pedestrian orientation of buildings;

- Required transparency at ground floor level as well as on upper floors of new buildings;

- Density and height bonus for developments that provide active ground-floor uses;

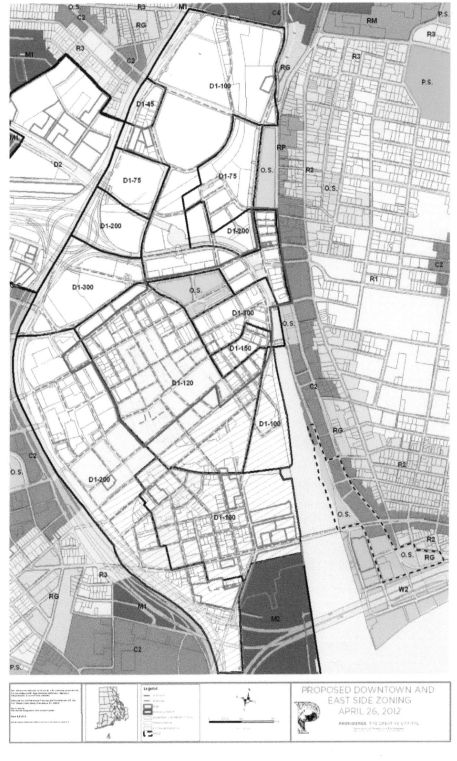

Figure 8.6: Revised zoning, adopted in 2012.
(Source: Providence Department of Planning and Development)

- Preservation of view corridors and designation of areas where height restrictions apply to preserve views.

A parking garage on Pine Street, built by Johnson & Wales University to serve its downtown campus, illustrates the effects of the increased attention being paid to the design of new buildings. Upper-level parking decks are horizontal, as opposed to angled, so the structure appears more like an office building than a parking garage. The first floor of the structure was designed to accommodate activity-generating uses, and the first-floor exterior of the building is covered with glass. Glass-enclosed stairwells lend a degree of transparency to the structure that visually, and perhaps reassuringly, connects people within the structure to those at street level.

Figure 8.7: New parking garage built on Pine Street by Johnson & Wales University.
(Source: Gene Bunnell)

Long-Envisioned Riverfront Park
Nearly Derailed by Proposed Ballpark

In February 2015, news stories broke that the Pawtucket Red Sox (the Triple-A farm team of the Boston Red Sox) had been sold to a group of prominent Rhode Island businessmen headed by outgoing Red Sox CEO Larry Lucchino. Soon thereafter, the team's new owners announced their intent to move the team to Providence, and build a baseball stadium along the Providence River.

Providence is only 50 miles from Boston, and heavily populated with Boston Red Sox fans, so the announcement was greeted enthusiastically by many Providence residents. In Pawtucket and elsewhere in Rhode Island the idea of moving the team was far less popular, because it would mean abandoning McCoy Stadium, the beloved ballpark that had been the team's long-time home. Pawtucket is only 10 miles from Providence.

Colorful renderings commissioned by the team and made public in April portrayed the stadium as a handsome addition to the city's riverfront. On May 12, 2015, the owners of the PawSox presented their stadium plan to the Jewelry District Association, which subsequently issued a statement that it was opposed to the stadium.

The team owners released the findings of a study (which they had commissioned) which projected that the ballpark could generate an estimated $12.3 million annually in indirect spending for the city and state, that "the state would receive $2 million in recurring tax revenue each year," and that Providence would receive about $170,000 in annual incremental tax revenue.

Over time, however, public reaction to the idea of building a baseball stadium along the Providence River became increasingly negative. The fact that the PawSox owners were seeking a state subsidy of $120 million, paid out over 30 years, plus an exemption from city property taxes, caused more than a few residents and elected officials to express misgivings about the project. It also turned out that the land on which the team wanted to build their stadium was the same 8-acre parcel of former I-195 land that had long been planned and set aside for a park.

In an op-ed article in *The Providence Journal,* Brent Runyon, Executive Director of the Providence Preservation Society, asserted that "plans for a signature waterfront park on the west side of the Providence River [had] been in place since 2006..." and that building a stadium on the site would "create a physical and visual barrier [to the river]" (Runyon 2015).

As more information became publicly available, it became clear that displacing the riverfront would have negative consequences well beyond the site itself. Back in November 2013, the I-195 Commission had secured a master environmental permit from the state's Department of Environmental Management (DEM), the Coastal Resources Management Council (CRMC), and Narragansett Bay Commission, whereby the agencies agreed to forego the need to conduct separate environmental reviews of each and every individual development project within the former highway corridor, but, rather, to treat development within the corridor *comprehensively.* The rationale for issuing the master environmental permit was the I-195 Commission's assurance that an 8-acre park would be developed along the Providence River, which would mitigate and filter stormwater runoff from development that was expected to take place elsewhere within the corridor. As explained in a May 2015 *Providence Journal* article,

> Builders are required to treat a percentage of stormwater on parcels they develop. However, if they can't meet the entire stormwater requirement on a parcel, the master permit allows them to gain credit from the parkland's treatment of stormwater (Bramson 2015).

The understandings and representations on which the master environmental permit were based would obviously no longer apply if a ballpark were built on the site of the proposed riverfront park. This, in turn, meant that it was going to be considerably more difficult for developers to complete projects on parcels of land elsewhere in the I-195 corridor that were slated for development; they would no longer be able to take into account the storm water runoff that would otherwise have been absorbed by the park. Instead, they would need to manage and treat storm water runoff almost entirely on their individual sites, which could significantly increase project costs. Nullifying the master environmental permit would also mean that developers would face much lengthier environmental reviews of their proposed projects, and that the outcomes of those reviews would be much more uncertain. "It ordinarily would take developers up to two years to get permits from those agencies, but the master-permit process [was] designed to take no longer than 60 days" (*ibid.*). Simply put, building a stadium on the land that had been reserved for a waterfront park was going to make it much more difficult to bring about economically beneficial development within the former 1-195 corridor.

On Sunday August 31, 2015, about 150 Rhode Island residents gathered on the I-195 riverfront parcel that was in dispute to send the message that "the land should be used for a public park, as it was intended" (Anthony 2015). That people would mobilize to protest the threatened loss of a riverfront park seems to have taken the team owners by surprise.

The owners of the PawSox also seem to have significantly underestimated the cost of building a stadium on the riverfront site—having apparently assumed that the land would be given to them at little or no cost. However, federal highway officials told state officials that if the PawSox went ahead with their plan to build a stadium on the land that was reserved as a park, the team would have to pay fair market value for the land—which would add millions of dollars to the project's cost. It also turned out that the waterfront park site was not really large enough to accommodate the stadium, and the team would need to purchase additional adjacent land owned by Brown University at a cost of $15 million.

Even if the I-195 Commission had wanted to facilitate the stadium project, there was one further complication. If a ballpark project went ahead, "the I-195 Commission would have to identify 14.7 acres for open space as part of a new land use plan" to replace the land previously designated as open space (*ibid.*).

On September 19, 2015, PawSox chairman Larry Lucchino announced that the team was ending its campaign to build a baseball stadium on the riverfront site. However, he insisted that continuing to play at McCoy Stadium after the team's lease expired in 2020 was out of the question. Relocating to another site in Providence wasn't entirely off the table, he said. "We will now begin to consider all other options and proposals we receive, including city officials' suggestions of potential other sites in Providence" (Benjamin Hill, 2015). Not long thereafter, news reports circulated that Worcester, New Bedford and Springfield, Massachusetts were under consideration as possible homes for the team.

Looking back at the riverfront stadium fiasco, it is hard to escape the conclusion that the team's owners didn't do their homework. They never apparently considered any other site other than the riverfront site. They simply cast their eyes on the waterfront land that had been reserved for a park and declared, "That's the one we want." The fact that building a ballpark along the river would violate the master environmental permit the I-195 Commission had secured for the district, and undermine prospects for achieving economically beneficial development in the I-195 District, also seems to have been something they overlooked.

The reason the team's owners took such a seemingly cavalier approach to the project may be that they assumed there would be such a groundswell of public support for the proposed stadium that state and city officials would see the political writing on the wall, and remove any and all obstacles that stood in the way of the project.

It remains unknown at the time of this writing where the franchise will ultimately end up. Other sites in Providence may yet be identified that could accommodate a baseball stadium for the PawSox. Meanwhile, many Rhode Islanders hold out hope that one way or another the PawSox can remain in Pawtucket.

The Huge Task of Relocating a Major Section of Interstate Highway

Ten years after the Old Harbor Plan calling for the relocation of I-195 was completed, construction finally began in 2002. While most of the construction took place within an entirely new highway right-of-way, a smaller but significant amount of construction needed to occur along the previously existing alignment, as in the area of the I-95/I-195 interchange, which remained active throughout the period of construction.

A key element of the project involved the construction of a new bridge that would carry I-195 traffic over the Providence River. To shorten the time that would otherwise have been required, the new bridge (which was designed by William Warner) was constructed off-site and floated 12 miles on a barge to where it was put firmly into place; this allowed the simultaneous construction of the bridge's concrete foundation.

Figure 8.8: Architect William D. Warner in front of new I-195 bridge he designed, prior to its being shipped by barge and put into place. (Source: Bill Warner's family)

In November 2007, realigned portions of I-195 handled their first traffic. By the middle of 2009, the newly aligned highway was fully open to traffic. In the fall of 2010, work began on removing former portions of I-195, and this was completed in the summer of 2011.

Relocating I-195 required the construction of 14 new bridges, 25 lane-miles of new interstate highways, new on- and off-ramps, and a new 1,200-foot-long, eight-lane mainline highway bridge over the Providence River. Handsomely lit at night, the new bridge has become a notable and distinguishing feature of the city's skyline. A 50-foot-wide bridge for pedestrians and bicyclists was also built parallel to the new highway bridge, along with 4,100 feet of pedestrian walkways and riverwalks. After the old I-195 was completely removed, new city streets also needed to be constructed, to reconnect Downcity and the Jewelry District after decades of being separated by I-195.

Figure 8.9: Aerial photo showing completed realignment of I-195, and the corridor of vacant land left behind after the old I-195 highway was removed. (Source: Maine Imaging, Providence Department of Planning and Development)

Developing the Knowledge District: A Work in Progress

In 2008, Johnson & Wales University renovated and converted the former Rolo manufacturing building in the Jewelry District into its Downcity Campus Student Services Center: a project recognized by the Providence Preservation Society as an "extraordinary and positive contribution to the livability and urban fabric of Providence."

Meanwhile, JWU sought to acquire two parcels of former I-195 land without having to go through the I-195 Commission, as provided for in the relevant legislation. JWU eventually paid the State of Rhode Island $3.9 million for the land, which the state used to pay for installing infrastructure and utilities within the I-195 Corridor. It should be noted that authorization for separating these two parcels from the balance of the former I-195 corridor, and for selling the two parcels to Johnson & Wales University without having to go through the I-195 Commission, was specifically provided in H5995, the 2011 act that established the I-195 Commission.

In April 2015, JWU began construction of a $40 million, three-story, 71,000 square foot building on one of those parcels, which will house the school's School of Engineering and Design as well as laboratories and facilities associated with its new biology program. The building was scheduled to be completed in time for the start of JWU's 2016 -17 academic year. Not far away in the Jewelry District, outside the former I-195 corridor, the former Little Nemo Jewelry Manufacturing Co. building was completely renovated into a 134,000 square foot, state-of-the-art facility for Brown's Warren Alpert Medical School.

Meanwhile, Johnson & Wales University renovated and converted another former jewelry factory just outside the former I-195 corridor to house its new Center for Physician Assistants Studies. Taking advantage of the center's proximity to Brown's Alpert Medical School, the two schools are collaborating by sharing professional resources.

One of the most highly anticipated projects underway in the Knowledge District is the $220 million South Street Landing project. This project involves the renovation, conversion, and expansion of the former South Street Power Station to accommodate an advanced nursing education program jointly oper-

Figure 8.10: Robert Azar, Deputy Director of Planning, leading a walking tour of the land within the former I-195 corridor in April 2016 and speaking in front of the new building under construction that will house JWU's School of Engineering and Design and new biology program. (Source: Gene Bunnell)

Figure 8.11: Brown University's Alpert Medical School building as viewed from Eddy Street in the Jewelry District.

Figure 8.12: This view, looking down Eddy Street alongside the Alpert Medical School building conveys a sense of the urban industrial character that formerly existed, and still exists in parts of the former Jewelry District. (Source: Gene Bunnell)

ated by the University of Rhode Island and Rhode Island College. The project will also house administrative offices of Brown University. A privately financed seven-story structure, with graduate student housing on the upper floors and restaurant/retail space on the ground floor, is also part of the project. The final component of the project, which was approved by the Providence Zoning Board of Review in February 2015, involves the construction of an eight-story, 740-space parking garage. Construction work on the South Street Landing project began in July 2015.

One possible reservation concerning all this university-related development is that facilities associated with educational institutions are typically tax-exempt. In that regard, it is important to note that before agreeing to sell a parcel of land for development, the I-195 Commission requires that a payment-in-lieu-of-taxes agreement (PILOT) be entered into with the City of Providence specifying the amount of money the owner/developer will pay annually to the city in lieu of taxes. PILOT agreements have already been entered into with the City of Providence by Brown University, Johnson & Wales University, and other institutions.

In July 2015, the Wexford Group submitted a development proposal for five acres of land in the I-195 District, calling for a hotel, housing, and a mix of laboratory/research/office space for the biological sciences. On December 14, 2015, the I-195 Commission authorized its executive director and chairman to execute a purchase and sale agreement with Wexford for parcels 22 and 25 (Nickerson, www.gcpvd.org December 18, 2012). During the same meeting, the commission approved the design plan for a mixed use development that will occupy a one-third acre parcel in the Fox Point neighborhood. The project, being carried out by Royal Oaks Realty LLC, will involve the renovation of the historic former Fuller Iron Works, as well as the construction of a seven-story building that will include apartments, office space, and retail space (*ibid.*). Meanwhile, an industrial building in the Jewelry District has been bought by Waldorf Capital Management LLC, which plans to renovate and convert it into 57 apartments, with ground-floor restaurant space. Martha Werenfels and Ed Cifune of Durkee, Brown, Viveiros and Werenfels are leading the design team for the project.

As the above-described activity suggests, interest in developing properties within the Knowledge District appears to be increasing. Nevertheless, it is important not to get carried away with overly optimistic expectations regarding how quickly the area will be developed.

The entire Knowledge District encompasses a total of 360 acres, of which 140 acres were vacant or underutilized as of 2012. To put these figures in perspective, the amount of vacant and underutilized land in the Knowledge District is roughly twice the land area that was available for development within the Capital Center project area. Development of Capital Center has been going on for over 30 years, and a small amount of land still remains vacant and undeveloped. Given this prior experience, it seems reasonable to expect that developing the Knowledge District could take every bit as long as Capital Center.

Taking a long time to develop the vacant/underutilized land in the Knowledge District may not be all that undesirable. Some of the most economically beneficial, high-profile projects came about fairly late in the process of developing Capital Center. The same could very well hold true in the case of the Knowledge District.

Chapter Nine:

Creating a More Transit-Oriented, Pedestrian-Friendly Downtown

Railroad Station Expansion and Transit Hub

Providence's railroad station is the fourteenth busiest in the U.S., serving Amtrak passengers traveling the Northeast Rail Corridor between Boston and Washington D.C., and equally large numbers of commuters riding trains operated by the Massachusetts Bay Transportation Authority (MBTA) between Providence and Boston.

Three decades after construction of the Capital Center project began, 15 acres of land remained vacant and undeveloped next to the relocated Providence railroad station. In November 2014, voters in Rhode Island were asked to approve a referendum (Question 6) authorizing the state to issue $35 million in state bonds to use that land to allow the railroad station to be expanded, and also to construct an associated multi-modal transportation hub: thereby enabling city bus routes to originate and terminate immediately adjacent to the railroad station. Grow Smart RI, a statewide environmental advocacy organization, actively supported the measure, arguing that the intermodal transportation center would create "more sustainable, environmentally-friendly ways for people to get around." Also supporting a "yes" vote on Question 6 was Move RI Forward, a coalition of business groups, labor unions, construction and real estate firms, and environmental and transit advocacy groups.

Other arguments for constructing the railroad station transit hub were that it would:

- serve as a gateway to downtown Providence and the rest of the state;

- re-establish a connection between train and bus service in Providence that was lost when the Amtrak station was moved to its current location, away from its former home in Union Station next to the Kennedy Plaza RIPTA hub; and

- allow buses to be relocated from Kennedy Plaza to the new railroad station transit hub, thereby freeing up space in Kennedy Plaza for public use.

Question 6 was approved. In addition to expanding the railroad station and constructing the multi-modal transportation hub, the funding authorized through the referendum will also pay for construction of a new railroad station/transit hub parking garage and for the reconstruction of the plaza leading to the railroad station, which had deteriorated badly over the years.

The railroad station transit hub project presents some interesting opportunities, given its proximity to Providence Place, the convention center, and the Omni Hotel towers. "The tracks leading in and out of the Providence train station pass directly underneath Providence Place. The two underground station platforms (one for Amtrak, the other used by the MBTA) end approximately at the edge of the Francis Street Bridge adjacent to the mall" (Orenstein, 2015 int.). One design alternative considered by RIDOT, according to Orenstein, was the possibility of providing a direct connection between the station platform and Providence Place, thereby enabling arriving passengers to directly enter the mall, and walk from there to the hotel and convention center without ever having to go outside—which would be particularly welcome during winter months (*ibid.*). At this writing, it is unclear whether this connection between the railroad station and the mall will be included in the final project plans.

Re-Imagining Kennedy Plaza

Kennedy Plaza is the center of our downtown, the front door to City Hall, and one of the first areas a visitor sees in our capital city... Our aim is nothing less than to reinvent and redefine our city's center... and change the way people think about the plaza by transforming it into a beautiful and usable space cherished by Rhode Islanders and visitors from near and far....
— Vision Statement, Downtown Providence Parks Conservancy

We relocated the rivers, the train tracks, and the highway. This is the next step. This is our generation's big revitalization.
— Cliff Wood, Executive Director,
Downtown Providence Parks Conservancy

Kennedy Plaza wasn't always used as the city's main bus transit hub. A 1959 *Providence Journal* photo looking southwest down the length of what was then

Figure 9.1: Providence City Hall, as viewed from Burnside Park in April 2016.
(Source: Gene Bunnell)

known as Exchange Place, with City Hall in the background, shows a tree-lined square with extensive plantings and landscaping.

Kennedy Plaza was converted into a transit mall around 1985, placing the city's main bus transfer hub adjacent to the Providence's Union Station, in apparent hopes of making it easy to transfer from bus to rail and vice versa. However, around the time the transit mall was being developed, the railroad tracks through Providence were being relocated, and a new railroad station was being built farther from Kennedy Plaza. The new railroad station opened in 1986. The need to better integrate rail and bus transit service became even more obvious when the Providence Convention Center was built on the site formerly occupied by the city's inter-city bus terminal, forcing private bus companies (such as Bonanza and Peter Pan) to move their operations to a fringe location.

Years before plans for the railroad station/transit hub reached an advanced stage, civic-minded individuals and organizations (such as the Providence Foundation) began laying the groundwork for reclaiming and re-purposing space in Kennedy Plaza. Two individuals who played key roles in this regard were Arnold "Buff" Chace, and Cliff Wood, Deputy Majority Leader of the

Providence City Council from 2007 to 2010. Another person who was involved early on was Dan Baudouin, Executive Director of the Providence Foundation.

The process of re-thinking how Kennedy Plaza should be used began around 2007, when Mayor David Cicilline initiated a series of public discussions aimed at generating ideas for improving and making better use of Kennedy Plaza. The impact of transit buses on the plaza was not the only issue up for discussion; another issue was the growing public perception that the plaza was not being adequately maintained and policed, and that people were often exposed to conditions and uncivil behavior that made them feel uncomfortable and insecure. "The meetings were held monthly, and were generally attended by 40-50 people," said Cliff Wood (int.). "People who attended the meetings learned about cities which had established parks conservancies because public spaces were not being adequately cared for" (*ibid.*).

In February 2008, Fred Kent and designers and planners from the New York City-based Project for Public Spaces (PPS) were brought to Providence to conduct a placemaking workshop titled "Rethinking Greater Kennedy Plaza."[39] Buff Chace paid much of the cost of bringing Fred Kent and PPS to Providence, very much as he did back in 1991 when he first brought Andres Duany to Providence. Other workshop sponsors included the Providence Foundation, the City of Providence, and the Rhode Island Public Transit Authority.

The 2008 placemaking workshop helped build public support for the Greater Kennedy Partnership (GKP) initiative. Not long after the workshop, representatives from the Providence Foundation, the Downtown Improvement District, and RIPTA began planning and sponsoring events aimed at drawing more people into Kennedy Plaza, such as Public Square Tuesdays, Farmers' Market Fridays at Burnside Park, and Rhythm and Soul Sundays with performances of live music. At the time, GKP lacked the resources to hire full-time staff, and depended on volunteers and contributions from partner organizations. Cliff Wood, who had taken on a leading role in the Kennedy Plaza initiative, was provided office space, and was being paid, at the time, by Cornish Associates. Wood's previous employment as Director of the Providence Department of Art, Culture + Tourism (2003-2006) helped him gain the support of arts and culture-related entities for the Kennedy Plaza initiative.

In 2011, GKP changed its name to the Downtown Providence Parks Conservancy (DPPC). "The idea [behind the name change] was to convey that the focus on Kennedy Plaza was one part of a much larger effort" (Wood, int.).

In 2012, Cliff Wood began working full-time as DPPC's Executive Director and DPPC became officially part of the Providence Foundation. That same year, Wood and DPPC helped put together a successful grant application to the

National Endowment for the Arts, which secured a $200,000 "Our Town" grant on behalf of the Providence Department of Art, Culture + Tourism to develop a long-term vision for expanding arts programming at Kennedy Plaza. The "Our Town" grant was used to hire Union Studio Architecture and Community Design of Providence to prepare preliminary design plans exploring the potential of Kennedy Plaza to accommodate a wide range of activities. Among the possible activities and attractions considered were: "a café, open market, water garden ... bicycle rental station, bocce, chess tables and carousel ... as well as "spots for reading, art, music, dancing, parties, weddings, food trucks and a movie night...." (Pina 2013).

The above-mentioned NEA grant also paid for some specific additions to Burnside Park, such as a storytelling fence and partial replica of an historic ship. Prior to these additions being made there was little activity in Burnside Park. "It now regularly has children's story hours and other events, such as the Summer Solstice series—including one which showcased Providence Police Chief Hugh Clements as guest disc jockey DJ Five-Oh" (Wood, as quoted by Pina, *ibid.*). The remainder of the NEA grant was used to finance an Arts Festival in the plaza in September 2012.

After a series of design studies by Union Studio, and months of meetings with RIPTA, various public agencies and departments, representatives of the business community, arts-related arts organizations, and local colleges and universities, the preliminary outlines of a long-term vision for Kennedy Plaza began to emerge. In April, 2013, Cliff Wood gave a well-attended public presentation of that vision in the Ballroom of the Providence Biltmore Hotel. Governor Lincoln Chafee and Mayor Angel Taveras hosted the event, joined by Honorary Chairmen U.S. Senators Jack Reed and Sheldon Whitehouse, and U.S. Representatives James Langevin and David Cicilline, the former Providence mayor.

In his presentation, Wood showed how the number of bus berths could be significantly reduced, to as few as ten; how bus lanes could be relocated to the edge of the plaza; and how space previously taken up by bus-only lanes could be re-purposed for public use. He also explained how an ambitious long-term plan for transforming Kennedy Plaza could be achieved incrementally in phases, as resources became available. To underscore this point, possible changes and improvements were broken down into nine sub-areas: Central Square; Civic Plaza; Market Square; Judicial Square; Bank of America City Center, Burnside Park; Biltmore Plaza; and the Gateway.

Wood was quick to point out that what he presented at the Biltmore "wasn't intended to serve as a formal plan," but to generate public discussion and interest in the overall project. After Wood's presentation, Mayor Taveras announced that the City of Providence would commit $1.7 million from a city transportation bond issue and join with RIPTA in funding the first-phase reconstruction of Kennedy Plaza: removing and relocating bus stops, eliminating bus-only lanes, leveling and resurfacing the plaza, planting trees, adding design features and amenities to create a more pedestrian friendly environment, reconfiguring traffic patterns around the plaza, and beginning the "Civic Plaza" section between City Hall and the RIPTA station. Soon thereafter, the City of Providence and RIPTA hired Klopfer Martin Design Group (KMDG) Landscape Architects of Boston to prepare a detailed design plan for the first-phase reconstruction.

The "Civic Plaza" area in front of City Hall initially targeted for improvement has special significance in Providence, since it is where then-Senator John F. Kennedy made a major campaign speech in November 1960 to a huge crowd. Back then it was called Exchange Place. In 1963, after his assassination, it was renamed Kennedy Plaza in his memory. 2013 proved a crucial year for the Kennedy Plaza initiative: In addition to securing the needed public funding for the first phase reconstruction of Kennedy Plaza, DPPC secured a $395,000 grant from the Champlin Foundation to reconstruct the northeast corner of Burnside Park, adjacent to Kennedy Plaza, to create an inviting, well-lit walkway between the railroad station and Kennedy Plaza. In addition, the Providence Department of Art, Culture + Tourism (ACT) secured a second NEA grant, this one for $75,000, to transform Kennedy Plaza into a venue with several stages, enabling performances and installations to extend along the city's "cultural corridor" on Washington Street (home to Trinity Rep and AS220). DPPC and FirstWorks (a local arts and cultural organization) partnered with ACT in developing the programs proposed in the grant application. The event funded by this NEA grant was held in September 2014.

In January 2015, a ribbon-cutting ceremony was held marking completion of the $2.4 million first-phase reconstruction of Kennedy Plaza, a project which significantly reduced the amount of space taken up by buses. Electrical equipment was also installed to enable concerts and special events to be held in the plaza. Tree planting, glass-roofed shelters, and pedestrian-scaled lighting help create a more inviting and pleasant environment.

At the ribbon-cutting ceremony marking the plaza's reopening, Mayor Jorge Elorza, then in his third week in office, said that the improvements would "create a community space that is welcome to everyone." Cliff Wood, DPPC's Executive Director, echoed the Mayor's remarks, saying that the key to the success of any public space is serving "many different people with different needs and interests, whereas the old Kennedy Plaza served commuters alone."

Figure 9.2: This photograph taken in April 2016 from the 16th floor Ballroom of the Biltmore Hotel shows how Kennedy Plaza was partially reconstructed to increase the amount of usable public space. (Source: Gene Bunnell)

Figure 9.3: Young musicians performing in front of an appreciative crowd at Kennedy Plaza. (Source: copyright Christian Phillips Photography)

Kennedy Plaza and the "Superman Building"

Kennedy Plaza is all the more important because the plaza is the front yard of the iconic "Superman building," which looks directly out onto Kennedy Plaza. In 1928, when it opened, it was the tallest building in New England (26 stories) and housed the Industrial National Bank. In later years it housed the Bank of America, which renamed it the Bank of America Building. But for most Rhode Islanders and citizens of Providence, the building remains the "Superman Building" because it so clearly resembles the *Daily Planet* newspaper building in the 1950s Superman television series.

It is not just its association with the long-ago *The Adventures of Superman* television series that makes the building important. The "Superman Building" is also by far the most distinctive and recognizable feature on the Providence skyline.

Despite its presence and power as a civic landmark, the "Superman Building" lost its last remaining tenant (Bank of America) in 2013. Indeed, one of the most vexing urban planning challenges facing Providence today revolves around the question of what will happen to the "Superman Building."

In 2008, the building was bought by High Rock Development of Massachusetts for $33.2 million, with the intent of redeveloping and converting most of the building's 441,000 square feet into 280 rental apartments, with the lower floors and street level reserved for retail and office uses. To carry out that scheme, High Rock said it would need $75 million in public subsidies ($39 million from the state, $10-15 million from the city and $21 million from the federal government in the form of tax credits for renovating historic buildings). From the outset, obtaining such a large amount of state and city funding seemed highly unlikely; under Rhode Island's historic preservation tax credit program, no single project can receive more than $5 million in tax credits.

Angel Taveras, Providence's mayor at the time, was quoted as saying, "A city is more than just one building" (Abbott, 2013). But it is hard to imagine Providence without the "Superman Building."

For the "Superman Building" to remain vacant and lifeless would be a tragic waste of an important city asset, and undermine all of the good that is being done to revitalize Kennedy Plaza. Conversely, bringing this iconic building back to life will generate activity that further enlivens the plaza. The two planning challenges need to be seen as inextricably inter-related.

On May 5, 2016, more than 150 people, including leaders of the local business community and public officials, gathered inside the Superman Building and held a rally aimed at drawing public attention to the importance of getting something done with the building, which by that time had been vacant for

three years, and, more specifically, to underscore the importance of state financial aid for a proposed renovation project that would add 278 new development housing units. As Buff Chace put it, "the building isn't going to go away."

> Proponents of the redevelopment would like to see the Superman
> Building [sic] transformed into some type of mixed-use building,
> which would bring more residents to the downtown and help bol-
> ster the spending for businesses in the area. An emotional Chace
> … also argued that redeveloping such an iconic piece of real estate
> in the city's downtown could go a long way toward lifting the
> spirit of the city (Sherman, PBN 2016).

Figure 9.4: Kennedy Plaza is like the front yard of the "Superman Building", as shown in this photograph
taken in April 2016. (Source: Gene Bunnell)

Chapter Ten:

Factors Contributing
to Beneficial Outcomes

A Large and Varied Cast of Contributors

The many positive changes in Providence were brought about by the sustained efforts of many people and organizations, drawn from the both the private and public sectors. Leazes and Motte summed it up well when they wrote:

> New 'players' emerged in both the public and private realms ....
> [P]ublic and private actors surfaced who would stay active ...
> to see projects to their conclusion. Their relentlessness would
> become a hallmark of the Providence renaissance (Leazes and
> Motte 2004, 69).

That so many different actors contributed to Providence's revival suggests that one of the most important factors determining a city's ability to recover after an extended period of decline is the extent to which residents and civic leaders remain committed to trying to make their city a better place. A far-from-complete Honor Roll of Local Heroes (see Appendix II) provides a sense of the broad level of civic engagement that made Providence's turnaround possible.

Non-Profit Organizations

Many of the positive changes in Providence have been brought about through the efforts of private, non-profit organizations. In that regard, no non-profit organization has had a greater impact on Providence than the Providence Preservation Society (PPS), which celebrated its 60th Anniversary in 2016. Founded during a neighborhood-based effort to save the College Hill neighborhood buildings from being razed by urban renewal, the organization's aims broadened over the years to encompass and support preservation-oriented efforts throughout the city. PPS has been so successful in persuading citizens and elected officials of the importance of preservation that the reuse and integration of old buildings into the fabric of the city has become a central focus of the city's community and economic development strategy.

PPS hasn't simply advocated for preservation. It has taken a direct role in rescuing distressed properties, by establishing the Neighborhood Revolving Fund in 1980. In 2003, it assumed responsibility for administering the Downtown Revolving Fund. Financial and technical assistance provided by the staff of the PPS-affiliated revolving funds has cleared the way for hundreds of deteriorated buildings to be renovated and re-occupied, thereby helping to maintain the city's historic character. PPS has also sponsored forums aimed at promoting public discussion of land use issues and challenges facing the city, such as the 2013 Providence Symposium titled "Not Always Easy: Building the New Urban Experience."

A number of other non-profit organizations have also undertaken initiatives and activities that have considerably benefited and improved the city. In 2007, civic-minded citizens and representatives of the local business community formed the Greater Kennedy Partnership (GKP), for the purpose of reclaiming Kennedy Plaza as a valued and active public space. In 2008, GKP organized a placemaking workshop at which numerous ideas and proposals for redesigning the plaza were aired and discussed. In 2011, GKP changed its name to the Downtown Providence Parks Conservancy (DPPC), and Cliff Wood officially became the organization's Executive Director. In February 2012, Cliff Wood was provided with office space at the Providence Foundation and joined the staff of the Foundation, at which point DPPC became a fiscal agency of the Providence Foundation.

AS220, an artist-run, non-profit organization, oversees and manages a wide variety of arts-related activities and programs in downtown Providence. In the process it has made Downcity a much more interesting and appealing place to visit and live. As of 2015, AS220 had acquired and renovated three downtown buildings containing a total of over 100,000 square feet of space.

In 1996, yet another non-profit arts organization, *Waterfire* Providence, was created to take over responsibility for staging installations of *Waterfire* on an annual basis. With the benefit of broad-based private and public support; voluntary contributions from individuals, organizations, and businesses throughout the city and region; and the assistance of hundreds of volunteers, *Waterfire* Providence has kept Barnaby Evans' creation alive by making it a permanent fixture in downtown Providence. As of 2016, *Waterfire* Providence had staged *Waterfire* for twenty consecutive years.

Neighborhood associations have also made important contributions to improving the livability of various parts of the city. According to the Providence Office of Community Relations, there are fourteen active neighborhood associations in Providence (See Figure 10.1). One such neighborhood association, the Jewelry District Association, spearheaded planning efforts that focused public attention on what was going to happen to that part of the city after the old sections of I-195 were removed. In another part of Providence, the West Broadway Neighborhood Association (WBNA) has been remarkably successful in building a sense of community and in helping to create a sense of shared purpose in the city's west side. WBNA has also played in important intermediary role in enabling a large number of properties in the West Broadway and Armory neighborhoods to benefit from PRF rehabilitation loans, grants and technical assistance.

Enterprise and Success in Obtaining Foundation Support

Grants secured from the National Endowment for the Humanities (NEH) and National Endowment for the Arts (NEA), a number of them secured through the Providence Foundation, helped fund a number of exploratory studies and planning processes which expanded public understanding of what was possible:

- A $27,000 NEA grant helped pay the cost of preparing the 1974 *Interface Providence plan*.

- A grant secured in 1977 from the NEH enabled PPS to bring leaders of preservation initiatives elsewhere to Providence to explain how preservation had helped revitalize their respective cities.

- An NEA grant provided the funding for William D. Warner's 1983 Providence Waterfront Study, which produced the Memorial Boulevard Extension/River Relocation plans, which in turn led to the uncovering of the rivers through downtown Providence.

- An NEA grant award of $200,000 paid for the development of a long-term vision for Kennedy Plaza in 2012.

- A 2013 NEA grant award of $75,000 to DPPC, the Providence Department of Arts, Culture + Tourism and FirstWorks helped fund an arts festival in September 2014 that was centered on Kennedy Plaza and extended along the city's "cultural corridor" of Washington Street to Trinity Repertory Theatre and AS220.

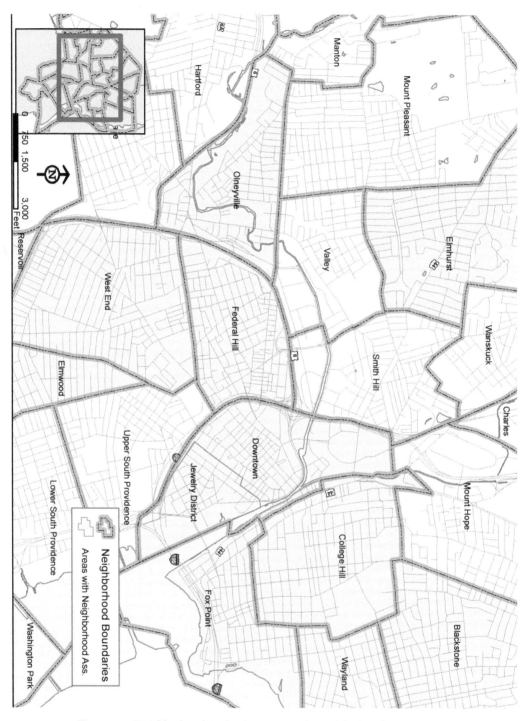

Figure 10.1: Neighborhoods in the Core Area with Neighborhood Associations.
(Source: Providence Department of Planning and Development).

Other foundation grants secured included the following:

- $150,000 challenge grant from the Rhode Island Foundation in 1980 to provide the initial capital for the Providence Neighborhood Revolving Fund—which was matched by a commitment of $300,000 of Community Development Block Grant Funds over five years from the City of Providence;

- $7.3 million in funding provided by the Rhode Island Foundation in 2003, thereby enabling PRF to take over responsibility for managing the Downtown Loan Fund;

- A 2012 ArtPlace America grant award of $454,000 to enable the non-profit organization Waterfire to "launch a public art incubator [and] create new art works and public programs...";

- A 2015 grant award of $395,000 by the Champlin Foundation to DPPC and the city to reconstruct the northeast corner of Burnside Park and create an inviting walkway between the railroad station and Kennedy Plaza;

- A 2015 ArtPlace America grant award of $300,000 to the Providence Department of Art, Culture + Tourism and Rhode Island Local Initiatives Support Corporation (LISC) to integrate arts and culture into the field of community planning and development, such as by funding an arts project called "Illuminating Trinity" and a "Community Innovation Lab" in the Upper South Providence neighborhood.[40]

Urban Planners and Designers

Professional planners and designers played key roles in Providence's transformation. For example, the College Hill neighborhood planning and preservation effort that began in the late 1950s benefitted considerably from the advice and guidance provided by architectural historian Antoinette Downing, planner Lachlan Blair, and architects Stewart Stein and William D. Warner. Years later, William Warner would play an even more prominent role in transforming the city by developing the bold plan that led to uncovering and relocating the rivers through downtown, and by following up on that success by convincing local, state and federal officials that I-195 should be relocated. "For more than a decade, William Warner spent many hundreds of billable, but never paid, hours showing the community the possibilities of Providence's long-neglected waterfront" (Orenstein 1997, B5).

Samuel J. Shamoon, the city's Associate Director of Planning, fortunately recognized that the original plan for Capital Center would have overwhelmed Memorial Square with traffic, and convinced the CCC that the plan needed to be revised to integrate with, and complement, the Memorial Boulevard Extension project. Architect Marilyn Taylor, who headed SOM's design team for the Capital Center project, deserves much of the credit for the design features and amenities that were incorporated into Waterplace Park that make it a unique and inviting public space.

The urban design charrettes Andres Duany conducted in 1991 and 2004 raised public awareness of how important it is that buildings frame and relate to streets and sidewalks—insights that underscored the need to revise the city's land use and zoning regulations. Encouraged by the positive public response to Duany's design ideas, planners from the city's Department of Planning and Development undertook a lengthy process aimed at building public support for revising the city's zoning ordinance, holding numerous meetings in neighborhoods throughout the city at which they explained the unintended negative consequences of the then-current land use regulations, and outlined zoning changes that were under consideration. It took a long time, but a substantially revised municipal zoning ordinance, incorporating many of Duany's recommended urban design principles, was eventually adopted by the Providence City Council in 2012.

The placemaking workshop conducted by the Project for Public Spaces in 2008 served an equally important purpose, encouraging attendees to re-imagine what Kennedy Plaza might be like in the future by presenting a wide range of design ideas and possibilities of how the square might be redesigned and reconfigured. Indeed, one of the most remarkable aspects of what has happened in Providence is the way outside planning and design consultants introduced new ideas and approaches that were eventually embraced and became standard practice.

City-State Relations

Rhode Island is the smallest state in the country, measuring only about 48 miles long and 37 miles wide, so it may not be surprising that state government officials and agencies played important roles in shaping plans and policies affecting the state's capital city. As one my sources put it, "In Rhode Island, everybody knows everybody."

When it came time to redevelop the vacant, underutilized land freed up by relocating the Northeast Rail Corridor, state legislation was passed authorizing the establishment of a 13-member commission (the Capital Center Commission) to oversee the development process—with the governor, the mayor of Providence, and executive director of the Providence Foundation each appointing four members. As further specified in the legislation, the chair of the commission was to be jointly appointed by all three.

J. Joseph Garrahy, Rhode Island's Governor from 1977 to 1985, played a key role in getting FHWA to approve William D. Warner's plan calling for the relocation of I-195. Garrahy recognized the importance of the project to Providence, and convinced FHWA's regional administrator Gordon Hoxie, an avid bicyclist and hiker, to sign off on the project (Leazes and Motte int.).

When it came time to redevelop surplus land freed up by relocating I-195, state legislation was once again passed calling for the establishment of a state-appointed commission (the I-195 Redevelopment Commission) to oversee the development process. In this instance, the legislation called for a seven-member commission, with all members appointed by the governor.

Perhaps the best way to illustrate the intermixing of city and state roles is by describing the backgrounds and intersecting careers of two key individuals: Joseph R. Paolino, Jr., and Bruce Sundlun. Before being elected governor 1991, Bruce Sundlun was president of the Outlet Co., which for much of the 20th century operated its flagship department store on Weybosset Street. Beginning in the middle of the 20th century, the company diversified by adding and acquiring stores elsewhere, and somewhat later by acquiring a number of television and radio stations in different parts of the country. Under Sundlun's leadership, the company sold the flagship store in downtown Providence along with all its other retail stores, and concentrated on its broadcasting and communications empire.

The Weybosset Street Outlet Co. store was sold in 1980 to another retailer. Two years later it closed, and in 1986 the block that housed the store was destroyed by fire. For a number of years there seemed little reason to believe that anything positive would happen on the derelict, contaminated Outlet Co. property. However, having set in motion the events that led to the demise of the Outlet Co. property on Weybosset Street, Sundlun made an effort to "make things right" when he became Rhode Island's governor (1991-1995).

As explained in Chapter Seven, one of the most important outcomes of Andres Duany's 1991 charrette in Providence was that Jack Yena, president of Johnson & Wales University, became willing to consider the possibility of locating JWU's main campus in downtown Providence, and building the campus on the fire-ravaged block on Weybosset Street formerly occupied by the Outlet Company. Nevertheless, he remained reluctant to move forward with purchasing the property given its environmental contamination and the substantial costs that would be incurred in cleaning up the site.

Sundlun called upon former Providence Mayor Joseph L. Paolino, whom he had named to head the state's Economic Development Corporation (RIEDC), to break the impasse and chart a way forward. Paolino was perfectly suited to play this role. Paolino's family had been long-time owners of downtown property, so he was naturally inclined to want to arrive at a solution that would rid the downtown of a festering eyesore. Also, one of the reasons Sundlun chose Paolino to head RIEDC was that he was regarded as being a good negotiator (Orenstein, 2015 int.). Paolino set up a meeting with representatives of JWU and the bank that owned the Outlet Co. property, and proposed the following terms: the State of Rhode Island would commit to paying for cleaning up and removing contamination from the Outlet Co. property, if JWU would commit to buying the property and building its campus there. JWU and the bank agreed to the terms, and a binding agreement was reached.

Stars in Alignment

The fact that Rhode Island's political stars were in near-perfect alignment made the expensive infrastructure that physically reshaped downtown Providence projects financially feasible. Rhode Island's six-term U.S. Senator, Claiborne Pell, who had a life-long interest in railroads, drafted the bill that became the High Speed Ground Transportation Act of 1965, which was aimed at improving rail service along the Northeast corridor between Boston and Washington D.C.[41] Pell's seniority in the Senate enabled him secure federal funding for relocating the rail corridor through downtown Providence, which in turn made the Capital Center project possible. Senator Pell also sponsored the federal legislation that established the National Endowment for the Arts (NEA), which may explain why Providence was so successful in obtaining a number of NEA grants—such as the NEA grant that funded William D. Warner's 1983 Providence Waterfront Study, which led to the Memorial Boulevard Extension/River Relocation project. Rhode Island's other U.S. Senator, John Chafee, helped secure the federal funding needed for the Memorial Boulevard Extension/River Relocation project.

The FRA paid the $33 million cost of relocating the railroad tracks and constructing a new railroad station. Relocating the rivers, constructing the highways and highway interchanges, and constructing Waterplace Park and the riverwalks, cost $136 million, most of which was paid for by the FHWA.[42]

Federal highway funds also paid for the construction of pedestrian bridges and underpasses, riverside walkways and pedestrian plazas, as well as design features and amenities that made the area visually attractive and inviting. The cost to the City of Providence was only $6 million—3.5% of the total combined amount paid by the FHWA and FRA.[43]

Chapter Eleven:

What Other Post-Industrial Cities Can Learn from Providence

It might be argued that Providence had some advantages other post-industrial cities don't have, which enabled it to turn itself around after decades of economic decline. As both the capital and largest city of a very small state, it was very much on the political radar of state elected officials. In fact, a number of state departments and agencies (such as RIDOT, RIDEM, RIPTA, RIEDC, and RICCA) played key roles in connection with major projects in Providence. Two special purpose state-established commissions were also created the Capital Center Commission, to oversee the redevelopment of the Capital Center project area; and the I-195 Redevelopment Commission, to oversee the development of the vacant land freed up by relocating Interstate 195. Rhode Island's government also gave a major boost to historic preservation and renovation efforts in Providence by establishing a state Historic Tax Credit Program to operate in conjunction with the federal Historic Preservation Tax Credit.

Lastly, as noted at the end of the previous chapter, Providence's "political stars" were in near-perfect alignment. This near-perfect alignment gave it an advantage in securing federal-level funding to advance its urban agenda. It enabled the Providence Foundation to secure a series of critically important grants from the National Endowment for the Arts, including funding for William Warner's 1983 Providence Waterfront Study, which produced the plan that led to the Memorial Boulevard Extension/River Relocation projects. The seniority of Rhode Island U.S. Senator Claiborne Pell, and his life-long interest in railroads, helped secure funding from the Federal Railroad Administration to pay for relocating the Northeast Rail Corridor through downtown Providence. Rhode Island's other U.S. Senator, John Chafee—who also had considerable seniority—helped deliver funding from the Federal Highway Administration, which paid most of the costs related to uncovering and relocating the rivers through downtown, as well as for the design features and amenities associated with the Memorial Boulevard Extension project.

Nevertheless, other cities hoping to achieve turnarounds of their own can learn important lessons from Providence's experience. Indeed, many of the approaches, principles and policies that produced beneficial outcomes in Providence could prove equally effective if diligently applied elsewhere.

Preserve Historic and Architecturally Significant Buildings and Districts

The first important step taken very early on was when residents of Providence's College Hill neighborhood got organized, secured the help of professional consultants, and developed the College Hill neighborhood preservation plan. Implementation of the College Hill plan prevented urban renewal clearance from spreading into that neighborhood. Restoration and renovation activities undertaken there eventually inspired similar efforts in other parts of the city.

There are a number of sound and practical reasons for encouraging the preservation, rehabilitation, and reuse of historic buildings:

- Preserving historic buildings and districts makes people feel proud, rather than ashamed, of their city's past. Preserving, restoring and reusing historic resources, and making them an important part of city's urban fabric and character, also strengthens local identity and sense of place. It makes a city authentic.

- Preserving historic resources is an especially powerful approach when a city's outlook for the future seems bleak, and when people have begun to lose hope that things will ever get better. When Providence hit bottom in the 1970s and 1980s, one of the most important things that the Providence Foundation and City of Providence did to raise the city's collective spirits was to rescue the Loews movie theater from being demolished, place the building on the National Register of Historic Places, and cobble together a combination of publicly- and privately-raised money to pay for the building's initial renovation. Given the desperate financial situation the city faced at the time, saving and renovating a cherished landmark that had been an important part of the life of the city for decades was by far the best investment that could have been made.

- Renovating and reusing historic buildings is a proven and effective strategy for community and economic development, as demonstrated not only in Providence's College Hill neighborhood, but also in other historic cities such as Charleston, South Carolina, and Savannah, Georgia.

- Renovating and rehabilitating old buildings is labor-intensive, and creates far more jobs per dollar spent than new construction. As a result, renovation and rehabilitation activity creates substantial spin-off benefits for the local economy.

Create an Entity Similar to the Providence Foundation to Provide Private Sector Leadership

One of the most important steps cities wanting to emulate Providence's successes could take would be to create a non-profit entity like the Providence Foundation. When economic conditions in Providence and, in particular, its downtown had reached a low point in the 1970s, the Providence Foundation was formed. Modeled after the Allegheny Conference in Pittsburgh, and composed of the presidents and CEOs of local corporations, banks, and public utilities, the Foundation often served as the catalyst that helped bring about beneficial policy initiatives and projects.

Not all cities' business leaders and private sector representatives are as civic-minded as those who came together to form the Providence Foundation. But if there *are* such publicly-spirited, constructively engaged private sector leaders, then forming a non-profit, non-governmental entity like the Providence Foundation would be an important first step. Leazes and Motte leave little doubt concerning the central role the Providence Foundation played in spurring Providence's recovery. "While there were and are many organizations that have [a] public-private nature and purpose within Providence, it is the Providence Foundation that was the key agency in the story of the Providence renaissance" (Leazes and Motte 2004, 72).

Time and time again, the Providence Foundation weighed in on pressing issues confronting the city, and urged city planners and local officials to aim higher and be more ambitious. For example, it was the Providence Foundation that hired the firm of C.E. Maguire to evaluate the feasibility of relocating the railroad tracks that ran through downtown Providence. The Maguire study concluded that relocating the tracks would cost about the same as reconstructing the existing track bed in its then current location, thereby removing the main objection to relocating the railroad corridor.

Think Long Range and Aim High

Make no little plans; they have no magic to stir men's blood and probably themselves will not be realized. Make big plans; aim high in hope and work, remembering that a noble, logical diagram once recorded will never die, but long after we are gone will be a living thing, asserting itself with ever-growing insistency.

— Daniel Burnham, Architect and City Planner

The 1909 Plan of Chicago, developed by Daniel Burnham, was full of "big ideas." Over a century after Burnham uttered his inspiring words, urban planning as practiced in all too many American cities seems to have become decidedly less ambitious. Contemporary examples of the bold thinking so much in evidence in Burnham's plan for Chicago are increasingly rare, which makes what has happened in Providence especially noteworthy. To achieve outcomes that are truly transformational, a city must be capable of envisioning and developing plans that will take years—perhaps even decades—to complete. Then it must obtain sufficient funding, and manage the implementation of such plans—and very possibly adapt them over time to new circumstances and opportunities.

Previous chapters of this book have recounted a number of instances when plan implementation in Providence was sustained over a remarkably long period. The large-scale infrastructure projects that reshaped downtown Providence took many years to carry out. The first iteration of the Capital Center plan was developed in 1979. Development of the surplus land freed up by relocating the rail corridor began four years later, in 1983; it has taken over 30 years to fully develop all of the land. As of 2016, a small amount of land within the original project area remains undeveloped.

William D. Warner's Old Harbor/Waterfront plan, which called for relocating I-195, was prepared in 1992. Actual construction work related to relocating I-195 did not start until 2002. It was not until 2011 that the new I-195 bridge over the Providence River was completed and the newly aligned Interstate began handling traffic. Redevelopment of the land freed up by relocating I-195 will likely take at least another ten years. Other than the massive "Big Dig" project in Boston, few public works and redevelopment projects in the U.S. have been as complex, and required plan implementation to be sustained over such a long period of time, as those in Providence.

Envision Possible Futures

Providence didn't tie its future to just one plan or vision of the future. Rather, Providence's vision of the future was progressively shaped by a series of plans prepared over the course of many decades, each of which contributed a distinct perspective and unique set of proposals. Needless to say, not all of these plans were implemented. Some were put away in a drawer and forgotten about for quite some time. Even so, worthy ideas and proposals in those plans often had an uncanny way of resurfacing years later—and when viewed in a new light and new context were often incorporated into plans that *were* implemented.

Cities seeking to learn and benefit from Providence's experience should devise highly participatory planning processes that encourage residents and other cultural and economic stakeholders to envision possible future outcomes, and then craft from the many perspectives a shared vision of a desired future. If their experience mirrors that of Providence, they will likely find that such planning processes produce a surprising amount of agreement regarding desired future outcomes. An additional benefit produced by such planning processes is that participants often become more engaged in helping to bring about those desired outcomes.

Analyze and Compare Alternatives

Much of the critically important transportation infrastructure on which American cities depend was built long ago and will soon need to be replaced. Many of the interstate highways and bridges that pass through and serve America's cities and population centers have already gone well beyond the date at which they ought rightly to have been replaced. In the coming years, American cities throughout the country will be confronted with the need to undertake major infrastructure projects and upgrades, not unlike those carried out in Providence.

When an interstate highway that runs through a city needs to be rebuilt, it should not simply be assumed that it should be rebuilt the same way, or even in the same place, as before. As Providence's experience so clearly demonstrates, alternative highway alignments and ways of reconstructing them should be identified, and the pros and cons of those alternatives, as well as of the existing alignment, should be analyzed and compared.

Federal and state highway engineers had originally expected that a new Interstate 195 through Providence would be built in the same location and manner as before. The idea of relocating I-195 might very well have been dismissed, had it not been for William Warner's Old Harbor/Waterfront study that showed that realigning the highway would free up a substantial amount of land for redevelopment, and open up riverfront space for other uses. A detailed comparison of the costs of the two alternatives also revealed that, because I-195 needed to be entirely rebuilt anyway, there was little cost difference between constructing the interstate along a new alignment and reconstructing it in its original location.

The need to rebuild and upgrade the Northeast Rail Corridor to accommodate high-speed passenger trains presented planners and engineers with an opportunity to make a similar decision: whether to rebuild the rail corridor where it had long existed, or relocate it. The initial assumption was that the rail corridor would be rebuilt in its existing location. But when a detailed study showed that it would cost about the same to move the corridor as to reconstruct it in place, planners and engineers supported the relocation plan.

Keep Chipping Away and Making Incremental Progress

Positive outcomes are sometimes not brought about by a giant leap forward, but rather, by continually making slow and steady progress. Providence's Neighborhood Revolving Fund (PRF) was created in 1980, and Clark Schoettle became the Executive Director of the Fund in 1983. Under Schoettle's direction, the PRF has typically provided financing to roughly 10 residential renovation projects each year—a number which may seem small. However, during the thirty-three years (1983-2016) Schoettle has directed the PRF, the number of renovated residential properties has grown steadily. As of 2016, the PRF had made $9.5 million in loans for 425 projects, and leveraged $110 million in private investment, thereby significantly reducing the number of deteriorated residential properties in Providence neighborhoods.

Make Good Use of Outside Experts, Speakers and Consultants

Sometimes the knowledge, insights and professional skills a city needs are possessed by people and firms right within that city. Cities all too often have made the mistake of undervaluing and failing to make good use of local professional expertise. Providence and state government agencies in Rhode Island did not make that mistake. Two of the plans that most dramatically reshaped and transformed Providence were developed by Rhode Island-based architect William Warner.

Much can also be gained by retaining the services of outsiders with wide-ranging experience: professionals who have worked in a number of different places, and/or who have in-depth knowledge of successful interventions and approaches in particular places. Outside experts and consultants can offer new perspectives leading to strategies and approaches that might not otherwise be considered.

On numerous occasions, outside speakers, experts, and consultants were brought to Providence. The Providence Preservation Society's experience in the 1970s illustrates the positive impact of outside experts inspiring a new course of action. In 1977, the PPS secured a grant from the National Endowment for the Humanities to bring experts from other cities to Providence to speak about how preservation efforts had helped revitalize various cities. Lee Adler spoke about the positive results brought about by Savannah's Preservation Revolving Fund, and Arthur Skolnick spoke about the preservation and renovation of historic buildings in Seattle's Pioneer Square Historic District. Inspired and energized by what they heard, PPS began to take the steps that led to the establishment of the Providence Neighborhood Revolving Fund in 1980.

In 1982, Brown University and the *The Providence Journal* sponsored a conference to discuss possibilities for reclaiming Providence's waterfront. James Rouse, whose company had developed Boston's Faneuil Hall Marketplace and Baltimore's Harborplace, was the conference's keynote speaker. Rouse told the assembled business leaders and citizens that the future of Providence could be assured by "going to the water." Rouse's speech generated a great deal of publicity in support of reclaiming Providence's waterfront, and helped boost support for William Warner's Old Harbor/Waterfront plan.

The week-long charrette conducted in Providence in 1991 by DPZ and Andres Duany also proved tremendously influential. At the charrette, Duany explained how Downcity's physical attributes and design qualities conformed to many of the fundamental principles of New Urbanism. Duany's underlying message was that a vital New Urbanist-style community could be created using Downcity's existing buildings and urban fabric as the basic raw materials. Arnold Chase, who had brought Duany to Providence for the 1991 charrette, must have been impressed and encouraged by what he heard, because within a few years his development company began investing in acquiring and renovating underutilized downtown buildings. An even more immediate by-product of the 1991 charrette was Johnson & Wales University's decision to develop a downtown Providence campus. It is impossible to overstate how important the addition of 10,000 students and hundreds of J & W faculty and staff has been in terms of contributing to the revitalization of downtown Providence.

Thirteen years later, Cornish Associates, the Providence Foundation, and the City partnered to bring DPZ and Duany back to Providence to conduct another week-long charrette in March 2004. The purpose of this charrette was to take stock of the progress the city had made since 1991, and identify the necessary next steps. Providence's Mayor at the time, David Cicilline, described the atmosphere that surrounded the charrette this way: "With each workshop, attendance grew. You could feel the energy in the room as people from all walks of life had the opportunity to discuss ideas about what Downcity should be" (O'Keefe 2006). Many of the requirements and design standards that Duany recommended at the charrette found their way into the revised zoning adopted in 2012.

One last example of Providence's use of outside consultants is worth mentioning. In 2008, a group of citizens and local business leaders that initially called itself the Greater Kennedy Partnership (GKP) joined with the Providence Foundation, City of Providence and Rhode Island Transit Authority to bring Fred Kent and the staff of the Project for Public Spaces to Providence to conduct a placemaking workshop titled "Rethinking Greater Kennedy Plaza." As a result of the workshop, citizens and elected officials gained a much greater appreciation of Kennedy Plaza's potential as a public space.

One of main impediments to reclaiming Kennedy Plaza as a public space was that over time Kennedy Plaza had become the main transfer point for city buses. As a result, much of the space in the plaza was taken up by buses that were standing and idling between runs. In 2012, Downtown Providence Parks Conservancy (the successor organization to GKP) secured a $200,000 grant from the National Endowment for the Arts to develop a long-term vision for expanding arts programming at Kennedy Plaza, and to prepare preliminary design plans exploring the potential of Kennedy Plaza to accommodate a wide range of activities. In 2013, Cliff Wood, DPPC's Executive Director, gave a public presentation of a possible vision for Kennedy Plaza to a large audience in the Ballroom of the Providence Biltmore Hotel. In the presentation, Wood showed how the number of bus berths could be significantly reduced, how bus lanes could be relocated, and how space previously taken up by bus-only lanes could be re-purposed for public use. After Wood's presentation, Mayor Taveras announced that the City of Providence would commit $1.7 million from a city transportation bond issue and join with RIPTA in funding the first-phase of reconstructing Kennedy Plaza.

Embrace and Apply the Principles of New Urbanism

Ever since Andres Duany and DPZ conducted their first charrette in 1991, Providence has served as a laboratory for demonstrating how a post-industrial city can be revitalized by thoughtfully applying the principles and ideals of New Urbanism. Given the important role that New Urbanist principles have played in Providence's resurgence, it is fitting that the Congress for New Urbanism chose to hold its Fourteenth National Conference (CNU XIV) in Providence in June 2006. "Given the conference theme [Developing the New Urbanism: Implementation], the rapid and ongoing transformation of 'Downcity' (Providence's downtown district) provided a wonderful backdrop for the largest CNU conference to date" (Lydon 2006).

DPPC and the Providence Foundation, city government and state agencies have striven to locally achieve two key aims of New Urbanism: a high quality public realm (at Kennedy Plaza), and greater use of public transportation and trains. DPPC's main focus, as previously noted, has been on restoring Kennedy Plaza to its former status as city's pre-eminent civic space. However, that objective could not be met as long as the plaza served as the city's main transit hub, with buses and bus-only lanes taking up much of its space. A new transit hub needed to be established elsewhere. RIPTA chose the railroad station as the location for the new transit hub, which RIDOT plans to expand to accommodate the increasing numbers of Amtrak passengers and MBTA commuters traveling in and out of Providence. Once the new railroad station transit hub is completed, a major impediment to more fully reclaiming Kennedy Plaza for public use will have been removed.

Quality Architecture and Urban Design

Yet another principle of New Urbanism pertains to the importance of striving to achieve high quality architecture and urban design, both of which are extremely important in strengthening a city's identity and sense of place. Again, an examination of Providence's experience provides evidence of considerable attention to design issues. As described in Chapter Six, one of the most important functions the Capital Center Commission served was to review and approve the design of every project proposed for the Capital Center project area.

A number of urban design-related provisions were also included in the revised zoning the City of Providence adopted in 2012, aimed at improving the visual and aesthetic qualities of the city. For example, the revised zoning sets "build-to" requirements to strengthen the pedestrian orientation of buildings, and prevents the spread of blank walls by requiring that the ground floors as well as upper floors of buildings be transparent. The revised zoning also offers a density and height bonus for developments that provide active ground-floor uses, and at the same time designates areas where building heights are restricted in order to preserve valued views.

A Final Comment

The citizens and professionals who came together over fifty years ago to try to preserve the character Providence's College Hill neighborhood probably never dreamed that their efforts would ultimately prove so successful. Likewise, the business leaders who formed the Providence Foundation, and the many other individuals identified in this book who played key supporting roles in trying to bring downtown Providence back to life, did not know ahead of time that their efforts would produce such dramatically positive results years later. There are no guarantees of success when it comes to trying to revitalize a struggling old city. If the citizens, elected officials and business leaders of Providence had been paralyzed by doubt and fear of failure, or hadn't had the courage to act affirmatively in the face of such uncertainty, the positive outcomes documented in this book would not have come about. It is this author's fervent hope that people in other cities who read this book will come to appreciate the power of sustained focus, incremental changes, courageous exploration of options, and collaboration among citizens, politicians, and the business community—and be inspired to aggressively pursue urban transformations in their own cities.

Appendix I:

Chronology and Timeline

1956-57   The Providence Preservation Society is founded and incorporated.

1959   *The College Hill: A Demonstration Study and Plan for Historic Area Renewal* is completed.

1960   The Providence City Council approves an ordinance creating the College Hill Historic District Commission. Construction begins on the Fox Point Hurricane Barrier.

1961   *The College Hill 1961*—progress after planning report is completed, documenting the progress that had been made in implementing recommendations contained in the 1959 College Hill plan.

         The Downtown Providence 1970—A Master Plan for Downtown Providence is completed.

1965   I-95 is completed and opens to traffic.

1966   The Fox Point Hurricane Barrier is completed, designed to protect downtown Providence against high tides and storm surges producing water levels 20 feet above sea level. Westminster Street is closed to traffic and converted to a pedestrian mall.

1968   I-195 is completed.

1974   The *Interface Providence* Plan is prepared by faculty members at the Rhode Island School of Design.

         Vincent A. "Buddy" Cianci, Jr., is elected Mayor. The Biltmore Hotel closes.

1975   The Providence Foundation is established

1975-76   Loews theater, now the Providence Performing Arts Center, narrowly escapes demolition.

1978   The federal Railroad Revitalization and Regulatory Reform Act is passed, providing federal funding for the Northeast Corridor Improvement Project.

1978-79	C. E. Maguire is hired by the Providence Foundation to analyze the feasibility of relocating the tracks through Providence and building a new train station.
1979	The Capital Center Plan document is completed by Skidmore, Owings & Merrill LLP. It calls for relocating the railroad tracks 600-850 feet to the north and for the construction of a new train station.
1979-82	The Capital Center District and Capital Center Commission are formed. The Biltmore Hotel re-opens.
1980	The Providence Revolving Fund is established.
1982	Brown University and the *Providence Journal* sponsor a conference to discuss possibilities for reclaiming Providence's waterfront. James Rouse is brought to Providence to be the conference's keynote speaker, and tells assembled business leaders and citizens that the future of the city can be assured by "going to the water." The Providence Foundation prepares and submits an application to the National Endowment for the Arts to obtain funding for William Warner's Old Harbor/Waterfront study.
1983	Construction of the Capital Center project begins. Architect William D. Warner conceives of and begins promoting the idea of uncovering the rivers that flow through the downtown. The West Broadway Neighborhood Association is established.
1984	Mayor Vincent A. Cianci Jr., pleads *nolo contendere* to assault charges and is forced to resign from office. Joseph R. Paolino, Jr., succeeds Cianci and serves as Mayor until January 1991. The Downtown Providence Historic District is listed on the National Register of Historic Places.
1984-86	William D. Warner's idea of uncovering the rivers gains acceptance. In the process of refining the plan and integrating it with the previously prepared 1979 Capital Center plan, Warner comes up with the bold idea of relocating the rivers.
1987	The new Providence Railroad Station is completed.
1988	The Rhode Island Comprehensive Planning and Land Use Act is passed by the Rhode Island Legislature, requiring each municipality to develop a comprehensive plan and adopt zoning regulations that conform to the plan.
1989	Design and Development Regulations are adopted by the Capital Center Commission, governing all subsequent development projects taking place within the Capital Center Project Area.

1991   Vincent A. Cianci, Jr., is re-elected as Mayor of Providence.

1992   The Old Harbor Plan, calling for the relocation of Interstate 195 through Providence, is completed and officially becomes part of Providence 2000—The Comprehensive Plan of the City of Providence. Architect and town planner Andres Duany and the firm of Duany Plater-Zyberk are brought to Providence to conduct a master plan charrette focused on Downcity Providence.

1994   Barnaby Evans' first installation of *Waterfire* in Providence takes place ("First Fire"). The Providence Convention Center is completed, along with its associated 261-room Westin Hotel and parking garage. The Downcity Providence plan is completed and adopted, and a new New Downtown Overlay Zoning District is adopted. New design standards and regulations are incorporated into the D-1 Zoning provisions to apply to the historic Downtown core.

1995   Providence Performing Arts Center's stage is expanded to accommodate Broadway shows.

1996   A second *Waterfire* event ("Second Fire") is staged. A non-profit 501(c)(3) organization, called *Waterfire Providence*, is established to be responsible for overseeing and making possible annual installations of Waterfire. A state-of-the-art sound system is installed at the Providence Performing Arts Center.

1997   The Jewelry District Association is formed.

1998   The Arcade and Grand Lobby of Providence Performing Arts Center are restored.

1999   Providence Place mall opens. Senator John Chafee secures highway funding for the relocation of I-195. The Providence 2000 comprehensive plan is completed. The Jewelry District Concept Plan is completed.

2000   The Rhode Island Foundation establishes the Downcity Partnership to manage a $10 million Downtown Revolving Fund.

2001   The State of Rhode Island establishes its own Historic Preservation Tax Credit program, and begins offering state historic preservation tax credits to properties and projects that qualify for federal historic preservation tax credits, thus providing an added financial incentive to undertake renovations/conversions of historic buildings.

2002   Vincent A. Cianci, Jr., is forced to resign as Mayor following his conviction for racketeering. The relocation of I-195 begins.

2003   After three years of operation, the Rhode Island Foundation transfers the $7.8 million remaining in its Downtown Revolving Fund to the Providence Revolving Fund, which takes over responsibility for administering the Downtown Revolving Fund in conjunction with its previously established Neighborhood Revolving Fund.

2004   Andres Duany is brought back to Providence to conduct a second charrette entitled, "Connecting and Completing Downcity."

2007   A cross-section of stakeholders come together to discuss possibilities for making better use of Kennedy Plaza. This loosely organized group calls itself Greater Kennedy Plaza. The Jewelry District Association and The Providence Foundation hire The Cecil Group, Economic Research Associates, and Maguire Group to prepare a framework study to guide future development of the Jewelry District.

2008   Fred Kent and others from the Project for Public Spaces are brought to Providence and conduct a Stakeholder Place-Making Workshop titled "Rethinking Greater Kennedy Plaza." The formation of the Downtown Providence Parks Conservancy is announced (replacing the previously named group called Greater Kennedy Plaza). The Jewelry District/Old Harbor Planning Framework Study is completed.

2011   The new bridge is put into place to carry I-195 over the Providence River and the newly constructed I-195 corridor begins handling traffic. Demolition of the former I-195 right-of-way begins. House Bill 5994 is passed by the Rhode Island General Assembly, establishing the I-195 District Commission to oversee redevelopment of land freed up by relocating I-195, and authorizing the Rhode Island Economic Development Corporation to issue bonds up to $40 million to finance acquisition of the land formerly occupied by I-195.

2012   Comprehensive rezoning of downtown Providence is adopted. Zoning regulations favoring warehouses and industry in the Jewelry District are eliminated. D-1 Zoning and design regulations that previously applied only in the Downtown core are extended to the Jewelry District and former I-195 corridor.

2013   Jan Brodie is hired as Executive Director of the I-195 Redevelopment District Commission.

2014   A "Tool Kit" is prepared and issued for developers interested in developing parcels within the I-195 District. Johnson & Wales University opens a new Center for Physician Assistants Studies in a renovated former jewelry factory adjacent to the I-195 redevelopment district.

2015   Downtown Providence Parks Conservancy (DPPC) and the Providence Foundation are awarded a $395,000 grant by The Champlin Foundation to create a pedestrian gateway within Burnside Park: a key step in the transformation of Kennedy Plaza. Johnson & Wales University begins site work on a new $40 million academic building on land formerly occupied by I-195, which will house the university's School of Engineering and Design and the College of Arts and Sciences' Biology Program. Construction begins on the $220 million South Street Landing project on the site of a former power station. Once completed, the project will house a joint University of Rhode Island/Rhode Island College-Advanced Nursing Education Program, Brown University administrative offices, privately developed student housing, and a parking garage.

Appendix II:

(Far-from-Complete) Honor Roll of Local Heroes

- John Nicholas Brown was personally responsible for the restoration of the John Brown House, which he donated to the Rhode Island Historical Society in 1941, and helped rescue the Providence Arcade from demolition in 1943. Mr. Brown was one of the principal founders of the Providence Preservation Society in 1956, and more than anyone else helped lead and guide the organization during its formative years.

- Beatrice Chace bought and renovated a number of dilapidated homes in the College Hill neighborhood when no one else was willing to do so, almost single-handedly helping stabilize and save the neighborhood.

- Joan Rich was PPS's first Neighborhood Coordinator, and helped expand PPS's preservation efforts beyond College Hill to other neighborhoods in the city.

- Mary Elizabeth Sharpe worked tirelessly to improve landscaping and parks in the city, helped create India Point and Jackson Parks, and helped establish a city endowment for planting street trees.

- Ken Orenstein worked in the 1970s for a non-profit group he helped to establish called Providence Citizens Lobby, which conceived of many of the revitalization projects that were adopted and funded by the Mayor's Office of Community Development (MOCD)—the new city department that was created by Mayor Cianci to administer federal CDBG and CETA (Comprehensive Employment and Training Act) funds that the City began to receive in 1975. Orenstein became Executive Director of the Providence Foundation in 1980 and served in that capacity until 1987. During that time, he played a key role in the decision-making process that shaped the Capital Center project.

- Robert Freeman made at least three highly notable contributions to Providence's revitalization. Originally trained as an architectural historian, Freeman carried out the historic research and documentation that lead the Loews Theater to be listed on the National Register of Historic Places, which enabled the City of Providence to use federal Community Development Block Grant funds to renovate the building. Freeman also played an important role in advancing the idea of relocating the rail corridor through downtown Providence. When it became known that the federal government was going to upgrade the Northeast Rail Corridor to accommodate high-speed trains, Freeman attended a 1978 meeting with the city's chief of planning, the chief of the planning division of the Rhode Island Department of Transportation, and the Executive Director of the Providence Foundation, who at the time was Romolo Marsella. Freeman pulled out a copy of the 1961 Downtown Providence plan and said, "Why don't we think about relocating the tracks? Maybe now is the time to do it." Then, in 1991, two years after he himself had become the Executive Director of the Providence Foundation, Freeman prepared the grant application that secured NEA funding for William Warner's Old Harbor study, which led to the decision to relocate Interstate 195. Sadly, Freeman's tenure as Executive Director of the Providence Foundation was cut short when he died in 1992 of lung cancer (even though he didn't smoke).

- Dan Baudouin became Executive Director of the Providence Foundation after the death of Robert Freeman. As of 2016, he had served in that position for 24 years.

- Barnaby Evans created *Waterfire*, which has become a defining and uniquely alluring feature of Providence. What began as an art project has evolved over time into an annual activity that attracts about 1.1 million people to Providence each year: generating $114.3 million in visitor spending, creating jobs, and generating substantial tax revenue for the City of Providence and State of Rhode Island.

- Umberto Crenca spearheaded the formation of AS220, the organization of artists which has had a remarkably positive impact in terms of making downtown Providence a more lively and appealing place to live and work.

- Architect Steve Durkee served on the Providence Planning Commission for seventeen years (including eleven years as its chairman) and has been the architect for a number of Cornish Associates' downtown renovation projects.

- Vincent "Buddy" Cianci, Jr., served 21 years in office as Mayor of Providence, a period of time that coincided with a stunning re-shaping and transformation of downtown Providence. Despite his apparent personal failings and perplexing behavior at times, Cianci deserves as much credit as anyone for the positive changes that were brought about while he was the city's Chief Executive. He also deserves credit for his strong and unwavering support for historic preservation, which is why the Providence Preservation Society in 2006 honored and included him in its 50th Anniversary Hall of Fame. As stated by PPS, "He recognized the importance of historic preservation to community rebirth as no other mayor before him had. Mayor Cianci worked to awaken the city's sometimes sleepy citizenry to the virtues and economic impact of historic preservation."

- Jack Yena, as President of Johnson & Wales University's Providence campus (1989-2004), accepted and acted upon Andres Duany's advice, and took the bold step of advising JWU to purchase the former Outlet Co. property and build a new campus in the center of downtown.

- Deming Sherman has been Chairman of the Capital Center Commission since 2011, a member of the commission's Design Review Committee 2009-2011, Trustee of the Providence Preservation Society (1990-2004), President of PPS (1996-1999), and Director of Grow Smart Rhode Island (1998-2013).

- Cliff Wood was a founding member of the Greater Kennedy Partnership and first Executive Director of the Downtown Providence Parks Conservancy; prior to that he directed the city's Department of Art, Culture + Tourism (2003-2006) and served on the Providence City Council (2007-2010).

- Clark Schoettle has directed the Neighborhood Revolving Fund for since 1983 and has directed the Downtown Revolving Fund since PRF assumed responsibility for managing it in 2003.

• What Beatrice Chace did for the College Hill neighborhood long ago, Buff Chace, the CEO of Cornish Associates, has done for downtown Providence: buying run-down old buildings, and renovating them. Chace's contributions to civic life have gone well beyond the renovation projects he has undertaken. It was Chace who was largely responsible for bringing architect Andres Duany to Providence in 1991 to conduct a four-day charrette, which led to Johnson & Wales University's decision to locate and build its campus in downtown Providence. Chace also was a key member of the group that formed the Kennedy Plaza Partnership, a citizen-led initiative whose purpose was to reclaim and revitalize Kennedy Plaza as a public space. To further that effort, Chace helped provide the financing that brought Fred Kent and the Project of Public Spaces to Providence to conduct a "placemaking workshop" in 2008, at which wide-ranging ideas and proposals for redesigning Kennedy Plaza were publicly discussed. Equally important, Chace employed Cliff Wood and provided him office space at Cornish Associates during GKP's formative years so Wood could work full-time on matters and issues GKP cared about. "Cornish paid me to work on behalf of GKP. It was something that Buff took on willingly" (Wood 2015, personal communication). The financial support Chace provided helped sustain GKP during those early years, and enabled it to mature to the point of becoming the non-profit organization now known as the Downtown Providence Parks Conservancy (DPPC). Indicative of the central role he has played in furthering the group's efforts, Chace is one of the seven members of DPPC's Executive Committee.

Appendix III:

Mayors of Providence, 1951-2016

Walter H. Reynolds (Dem.)	January 1951 – January 1965
Joseph A. Doorley, Jr. (Dem.)	January 1965 – January 1975
Vincent A. Cianci, Jr. (Rep.)	January 1975 – April 25, 1984; forced to resign, pleaded *nolo contendere*
Joseph R. Paolino, Jr. (Dem.)	April 25, 1984 – January. 1991
Vincent A. Cianci, Jr. (Ind.)	January 1991 – September 6, 2002; forced to resign following conviction for racketeering
John J. Lombardi (Dem.)	September 6, 2002 – January 6, 2003
David Cicilline (Dem.)	January 6, 2003 – January 3, 2011
Angel Taveras (Dem.)	January 3, 2011 – January 5, 2015
Jorge Elorza (Dem.)	January 5, 2015 –

Appendix VI:

Governors of Rhode Island, 1951-2016

Dennis J. Roberts (Dem.)	January 1951 – 1959
Christopher Del Sesto (Rep.)	January 1959 – 1961
John A. Notte, Jr. (Dem.)	January 1961 – 1963
John Chafee (Rep.)	January 1963 – 1969
Frank Licht (Dem.)	January 1969 – 1973
Philip Noel (Dem	January 1973 – 1977
J. Joseph Garrahy (Dem.)	January 1977 – 1985
Edward DiPrete (Dem.)	January 1985 – 1991
Bruce Sundlun (Dem.)	January 1991 – 1995
Lincoln Almond (Rep.)	January 1995 – 2003
Lincoln Chafee (Dem.)	January 2011 – 2015
Gina Raimondo (Dem.)	January 2015 –

Appendix V:

Executive Directors of the Providence Foundation, 1975-2016

1975	Joseph Madonna
1975 - 1979	Romolo Marsella
1980 – 1987	Ken Orenstein
1987 – 1988	Arthur Markos
1989 – 1992	Robert Freeman
1992 – 2016	Daniel Baudouin

References

Abbott, Elizabeth. "Providence, R.I., Is Building on a Highway's Footprint." *The New York Times*, August 19, 2015, p. B7.

Barry, Dan. "Vincent Cianci, Beloved and Scorned as Mayor of Providence, Dies at 74." *The New York Times*, January 29, 2016.

Bramson, Kate. "Proposed Pawsox stadium in Providence threatens master plan for stormwater mitigation." *Providence Journal.com*, May 2, 2015.

Bunnell, Gene 2002. *Making Places Special: Stories of Real Places Made Better by Planning.* Chicago, IL: APA Planners Press.

Cady, John Hutchins 1957. *The Civic and Architectural Heritage of Providence, 1636-1950.* Providence R.I.: The Book Shop.

Conley, Patrick T. and Paul R. Campbell. 1982. *Providence: A Pictorial History.* Norfolk VA: Donning Co.

Conley, Patrick T. and Paul R. Campbell. City Archives/City History. www.providenceri. com (accessed 12/19/15).

Cook, Greg. "How to Respond to a Bad Review? AS220's Bert Crenca Remade Providence." WBUR *TheARTery*, April 26, 2014.

Crenca, Umberto 2013. "Art and Craftsmanship in Service to Community." *TEDx Providence 2013.*

Fain, Barry. "Face Off at the State House: Are the Governor and the Capital Center Commission on a Collision Course?" *WPRI.com*, November 11, 2013.

Grimaldi, Paul. "Capital Center chairman opposed to more parking near R. I. State House." *Providence Journal.com*, October 16, 2013.

Hill, Benjamin. "Batting Around: PawSox look for new home." *MiLB.com*, September 29, 2015.

Leazes, Jr., Francis J and Mark T. Motte 2004. *Providence: The Renaissance City.* Boston MA: Northeastern University Press.

Lydon, Mike. "CNU at XIV: Coverage of the 2006 Congress for the New Urbanism." *Planetizen* June 7, 2006. (www.planetizen.com/node/20049)

Orenstein, Ken. "What agency played a key role in reviving Providence? The NEA." *The Providence Journal-Bulletin*, September 29, 1997.

Pina, Alisha A. "Transforming Kennedy Plaza: A Vision." *The Providence Journal*, April 18, 2013.

New Urban News. "Better places, stronger communities." http://bettercities.net/article/providence-charrette, April 1, 2004.

O'Keefe, Karen 2006. "At Home with a Vision." *The Town Paper*, Vol. 8. (www.tndtownpaper.com)

Pindell, Terry 1995. *A Good Place to Live—America's Last Migration*. New York: Owl Books, Henry Holt and Co.

Project for Public Spaces 2005. *How to Turn a Place Around: A Handbook for Creating Successful Public Spaces*. New York: Project for Public Spaces, Inc.

Project for Public Spaces."Rethinking Greater Kennedy Plaza: Placemaking Workshop Summary," February 27, 2008.

Providence Business News. "Cornish's Chace key player in downtown makeover," November 14, 2011.

Providence Preservation Society. *50th Anniversary Hall of Fame*. PPS 50th Anniversary Honorees at the historic Masonic Temple, March 31, 2006.

Runyon, Brent. "River site not suitable for ballpark." *The Providence Journal*, August 22, 2015.

Sherman, Eli. "Business leaders rally in support of Superman building." *Providence Business News*, May 5, 2016.

Smolski, Chester E. "Bringing it together, downtown." *The Providence Journal*, November 21, 1991.

Woodward, William McKenzie 2003. PPS/AIAri *Guide to Providence Architecture*. Providence RI: Providence Preservation Society.

Endnotes

1 Barry Bluestone and Bennett Harrison, 1982. *The Deindustrialization of America.* New York: Basic Books.

2 Publication of *Providence: The Renaissance City* (2004), by Leazes and Motte, reinforced the notion that Providence had experienced a renaissance.

3 In addition to the case study of Providence RI, *Making Places Special* included case studies of two other rustbelt cities: Chattanooga, TN and Duluth, MN.

4 A new Union Station was later built east of the first rail depot on land that was created by filling in the Old Cove.

5 Many of these businesses specialized in the production of jewelers' findings: the pin-stems, catches, hubs, dies, and other hardware for pins, earrings, necklaces and novelties.

6 For many years after the Great Depression, Providence's jewelry industry specialized in manufacturing costume jewelry.

7 The J. Walter Wilson Laboratory (1961) is a good example of the kind of building that intensified the impression that Brown University felt no need to "fit in" or respect the historic character and scale of the College Hill area. Woodward's *Guide to Providence Architecture* describes the Wilson Laboratory as "an affront to the neighborhood" (Woodward 2003, p. 174). Yet another example is the List Art Center (1971), designed by star architect Philip Johnson, which Woodward's *Guide to Providence Architecture* describes as follows: "Distinguished by its colossal 'colonnade' and saw-tooth roofline, the building is better as an object than as a neighbor in an historic district..." (*ibid.,* 165).

8 While many people were involved in the citizen-initiated planning effort that saved College Hill, the leadership of John Nicholas Brown over a 23-year period was absolutely critical to the success of the overall effort. In addition to being an original founder of the Providence Preservation Society, John Nicholas Brown was the society's chairman from 1956 to 1979. Brown's roots in the College Hill neighborhood went deep. He was a member of the family after which Brown University was named, and could trace his ancestry back to a follower of Roger Williams, who was with Williams in 1636 when Providence was first settled.

9 In 1978, the American Society of Planning Officials and the American Institute of Planners merged to create the American Planning Association.

10 Among the cities studied and, in some cases, visited first-hand, were: Annapolis, Maryland; Boston, Massachusetts; Charleston, South Carolina; Nantucket, Massachusetts; New Castle, Delaware; New Orleans, Louisiana; Newport, Rhode Island; Philadelphia, Pennsylvania; Salem, Massachusetts; San Antonio, Texas; Santa Fe, New Mexico; Savannah, Georgia; Washington, DC; Williamsburg, Virginia; and Winston-Salem, North Carolina. Learning how a comprehensive survey of almost 1,200 historic properties was carried out

in Charleston, South Carolina in 1941 was particularly helpful, and had a considerable influence on how the survey of historic properties was carried out at College Hill. In the Charleston survey, structures were classified into four historical periods and into five groups according to importance.

[11] Antoinette F. Downing moved to Providence from New Mexico in 1936. Perhaps because she was an "outsider" and looked at the city with fresh eyes, she recognized more quickly than many long-time residents the preciousness of the area's historic and architectural resources. Her reputation as an expert in historic preservation was first established when she wrote *Early Homes of Rhode Island* (1937). Her stature in the field of historic preservation was further strengthened by the publication of *The Architectural Heritage of Newport, Rhode Island: 1640-1915* (1952, first edition), which she co-authored with Vincent J. Scully, Jr. A founder of the Providence Preservation Society in 1956, Ms. Downing was also the founder of Stop Wasting Abandoned Properties (SWAP), and was the first chairman of the Rhode Island Historical Preservation Commission when it was established in 1967.

[12] Wendy Nicholas served as PPS Executive Director from 1981 to 1993.

[13] The easement gives the Revolving Fund the authority to take an owner to court and step in to take corrective action.

[14] The Revolving Fund doesn't typically impose such deed restrictions on homeowners who receive renovation loans, although it may impose a 10-year historic preservation easement to protect against improper renovations.

[15] The title of the plan, *Downtown Providence 1970—A Master Plan for Downtown Providence*, may be a source of some confusion. The plan was prepared in 1961, but was prepared in order to show what Providence could be like in 1970.

[16] The Providence Foundation was the official applicant for this NEA grant, which in turn financed the preparation of the RISD *Interface Providence Plan*.

[17] The federal Community Development Block Grant program was established by the Housing and Community Development Act of 1973. The City of Providence began receiving CDBG funds in 1974.

[18] The Providence Foundation was modeled after the Allegheny Conference in Pittsburgh, but was also inspired by "The Vault" in Boston: a group of powerful and influential members of the city's business community who met regularly, but privately, at the Boston Safe Deposit Bank during the 1970s to develop policy positions and chart strategies pertaining to public issues.

[19] Freeman went on to become Executive Director of the Providence Foundation from 1989 to 1992.

[20] This alternative, which Wilbur Smith Associates called Alternative #6, was included for evaluation as Alternative C in the Memorial Boulevard Extension EIS.

[21] The City of Providence committed $25,000 of Community Development Block Grant funds

to the study, "even as [its] own staff voiced some doubts" (Leazes and Motte, 2004, 113).

[22] According to Bill Warner, Edward Sanderson (Executive Director of the Rhode Island Historical Preservation Commission and a member of the Providence Waterfront Study Design Review Committee) was the person who came up with the idea of relocating the World War I memorial from Memorial Square to the park in front of the courthouse. However, the idea of relocating the World War I memorial to the 2-acre park near the courthouse, which already had a statue honoring the Italian explorer Verrazano, sparked opposition from two major segments of the city's population. Italian-Americans didn't want to share the site with a monument honoring veterans. Veterans' organizations, in turn, didn't like the idea of a monument honoring fallen American soldiers sharing the same square with another memorial honoring a person representing a country that had fought against American soldiers in World War II. Mayor Cianci convinced the Italian-American community to soften their objections. He also convinced veterans groups that the World War I memorial would not be diminished by sharing the space with a memorial honoring a courageous Italian explorer. In the years that followed the relocation of the WWI Memorial, other memorials have been added to the park, including monuments and memorials to the Korean War and Holocaust.

[23] http://waterfire.org/about/barnaby-evans-artist

[24] Of the $9.3 million in state and city sales taxes collected each year as a result of *Waterfire*, $8.9 million has gone to the State of Rhode Island, and $415,000 to the City of Providence.

[25] The soundtrack for *Waterfire* changes somewhat from year to year but, according to Waterfire Providence's website: "often returns to works by four principal composers—the Estonian composer Arvo Pärt's modern interpretations of ancient Christian and Russian Orthodox liturgical music; the American folk melodies played by Djivan Gasparyan on the Duduk or Nay (an Armenian oboe); the American avant-garde composer David Hykes' settings of various religious music for small chorus using vocal techniques derived from Tibetan 'overchanting'; and selections from Nicholas Lens' brilliant work *Flamma Flamma—The Fire Requiem*" (http://waterfire.org/about/music-of-waterfire).

[26] As a result of a 2015 merger, the name of the corporation was changed to IGT.

[27] The convention center hotel is now part of the Omni hotel chain.

[28] In Rhode Island, the state is the only government entity that is authorized to levy and collect sales taxes.

[29] Yena was JWU's President from 1989 to 2004. Having worked at JWU in various positions over 27 years before becoming university president. When Yena began as university president in 1989, the school was focused primarily on Business, Hospitality, and Culinary Arts.

[30] The building where the charrette was held was eventually acquired by Johnson & Wales University and became part of its campus.

[31] The Outlet Company was established in 1891. For years, its store on Weybosset Street

was its flagship location. In the mid-20th Century, the Outlet Co. expanded by opening stores in suburban locations and buying stores in the Philadelphia and New Haven areas, as well as in the Midwest. Under the leadership of its then-president Bruce Sundlun, the Outlet Co. acquired a number of television and radio stations in different parts of the country, and was transformed from being primarily a retail company to a broadcasting empire. In 1980 the company decided to leave the retail business entirely, and sold its downtown Providence store along with its other stores.

[32] The modern design of the former Broadcast House, now renamed Yena Hall, differs markedly from the classically-influenced design of the new buildings JWU has built on its downtown campus. The stark, unembellished, sharp-angled exterior of the former Broadcast House was dictated by Bruce Sundlun "to match his forceful personality" (Yena 2016 personal communication).

[33] Properties in Rhode Island are assessed at full value, which means the assessed valuation of any given property is supposed to approximate its market value.

[34] According to AS220's David Dvorchak, this photo of Bert Crenca accompanied an article written by Brian Salzberg titled "AS220" that appeared in the September 18th, 1989 issue of "The Works," an independent, Block Island arts magazine, which no longer exists (Dvorchak, personal communication). Bert Crenca isn't certain, but thinks the photo may have been taken by the artist Peter Boyle, who was involved with AS220 in the early years, but is now deceased (Crenca, personal communication).

[35] The Hurricane Barrier was built across the mouth of the Providence River to afford a degree of protection to the city from hurricane-driven storm surges like those that inundated and heavily damaged downtown Providence in 1938 and 1954. Construction of the Hurricane Barrier began in 1961 and was completed in 1966.

[36] Rhode Island's Secretary of Commerce, and the City of Providence Director of Planning are *ex officio* members of the I-195 Commission.

[37] Unlike the 2008 Jewelry District/Old Harbor Study, the 2012 Providence Downtown and Knowledge District Plan considered the Hospital District (on the opposite side of the relocated I-195 highway corridor) part of the Knowledge District.

[38] Funding for the city-wide re-zoning was provided by a U.S. Department of Housing and Urban Development Sustainable Communities grant.

[39] The Project for Public Spaces was established by William H Whyte (1917-1999), who conducted extensive studies and made films showing how people used public spaces. PPS specializes in offering training courses and educating communities on how to make public spaces more beneficial and welcoming. Insights and principles regarding how to create successful public spaces are contained in a 2005 PPS publication titled, *How to Turn a Place Around: A Handbook for Creating Successful Public Spaces.*

[40] The ArtPlace grant program, funded by the Kresge Foundation, is dedicated to the purpose of "creative placemaking" and "integrating arts and culture into the field of community planning and development."

[41] Pell served in the U.S. Senate from 1961 until 1997.

[42] The balance of the cost of constructing Waterplace Park was funded by RIDEM.

[43] The $169 million spent by the FHWY and FRA in 1985 is equivalent to $337 million in 2016 dollars. The $6 million spent by the City of Providence is roughly equivalent to $13.4 million in 2016 dollars.